What Does a Woman Want?

What Does a Woman Want?

READING

AND

SEXUAL

DIFFERENCE

Shoshana Felman

THE JOHNS HOPKINS UNIVERSITY PRESS

BALTIMORE AND LONDON

The Johns Hopkins University Press
2715 North Charles Street
Baltimore, Maryland 21218-4319
The Johns Hopkins Press Ltd., London

Library of Congress Cataloging-in-Publication Data

Felman, Shoshana.
    What does a woman want? : reading and sexual difference/Shoshana Felman
        p.   cm.
    Includes bibliographical references and index.
    ISBN 0-8018-4617-X (alk. paper).—ISBN 0-8018-4620-X (pbk.:
alk. paper)
    1. Feminist literary criticism.   2. Feminism and literature.
I. Title.
PN98.W64F32   1993
801'.95'082—dc20   92-47484

A catalog record for this book is available
from the British Library.

Contents

1

What Does a Woman Want?

The Question of Autobiography and the Bond of Reading

(Postface)

I must ask you to imagine a room . . . and on the table inside the room a blank sheet of paper on which was written in large letters *Women and Fiction*, but no more: . . .

A thousand questions at once suggested themselves. But one needed answers, not questions; and an answer was only to be had by consulting the learned and the unprejudiced, who have removed themselves above the strife of tongue and the confusion of body and issued the results of their reasoning and research in books which are to be found in the British museum. If truth is not to be found on the shelves of the British museum, where, I asked myself, picking up a notebook and a pencil, is truth? . . .

When a subject is highly controversial—and any question about sex is that—one cannot hope to tell the truth. One can only show how one came to hold whatever opinion one does hold. One can only give one's audience the chance of drawing their own conclusions as they observe the limitations, the prejudices, the idiosyncrasies of the speaker.

For in a question like this truth is only to be had by laying together many varieties of error.

—VIRGINIA WOOLF, *A Room of One's Own*

I

Difference and Truth

This is a book on love, desire, prejudice, confusion, "many varieties of error," insofar as they are all determined by the enigmatic truth of sexual difference. As the most contradictory human driving power, sexual difference is at once what separates and what attracts and brings together human beings; it draws us toward each other even while it estranges, threatens, and divides us. "It is precisely," writes Adrienne Rich, "*because difference is so powerful* (though the 'different' may be socially disempowered), that it seems the target of threats, harassment, violence, social control, genocide."[1] Sexual difference raises, thus, on the one hand, questions of desire, and on the other hand, questions of violence: the truth of difference is at once its power and its violence, and it is this power and this violence that the present book tries to understand.

But if, as Virginia Woolf suggests, the reality of sexual difference is inextricably tied up with "the strife of tongue and the confusion of body," if it cannot, moreover, be articulated as an answer that itself escapes the strife and the confusion, where, indeed, should we attempt to look for it? Could the literary work, or the psychoanalytic work, offer answers?

Toward the end of his career, Freud confessed that sexual difference was one question that, despite his work, remained unsolvable, at least for him:

> The great question that has never been answered and which I have not been able to answer, despite my thirty years of research into the feminine soul, is "What does a woman want?"[2]

What might it mean, this book will ask, for a woman to reclaim (reread, rewrite, appropriate) Freud's question? The answer, Freud acknowledged, was not available to him. It is not certain that the question has an answer. It is not certain that the answer—

if it exists—can become available to any man, or, for that matter, to any woman in our culture. But the question can be truly opened up and radically displaced, I would suggest, by being repossessed, reclaimed by women. It is the possibilities of this reopening and this displacement that the present study sets out to explore.

Reengendering the Question

Can literature in turn claim the question as its own specific question, and consequently be reclaimed by it? Can psychoanalysis? Is it in the power of this question to engender, through the literary or the psychoanalytic work, a woman's voice as its speaking subject? What consequences might such attempts at *en-gendering* a self-analytical female discourse have for the possibilities of reading, writing, thinking, analyzing, living, of women *and* of men?

This book proposes to explore these questions on the basis of close readings by a woman reader, on the one hand, of some women writers' autobiographical attempts (chapters 1 and 5), and, on the other hand, of three texts by male writers who dramatize, each in his own way, a male encounter with femininity as difference, a male experience, that is, of femininity as precisely the emergence of the (unexpected, baffling, and not always conscious) question: "What does a woman want?"

The male texts that consistently return to this central, though implicit, question are two literary, fictional stories by Balzac, "Adieu" (chapter 2) and "The Girl with the Golden Eyes" (chapter 3),[3] and one semiconfessional, semiautobiographical text by Freud (chapter 4), a psychoanalytic (referential) narrative that is, however, also crucially expository and exemplarily conceptual and theoretical: chapter 2 of *The Interpretation of Dreams*, which focuses on Freud's historic dream about his patient Irma. The practical and theoretical interpretation of this "specimen dream,"[4] as Freud entitles it, in fact lays the primary foundation for the whole theory of the unconscious.

These three male texts are obviously very different from each other in both form and content. All of them, however, can be thought of as love stories and, specifically, as narratives of failed love. The first and last (Balzac's "Adieu" and Freud's dream narrative) involve, moreover, a therapeutic project: in both, a woman must be cured but fails to be cured. In strange and very different ways both are, therefore, stories about healing. And in both, surprisingly and unexpectedly, healing turns out to be tied up with killing. There are differences, of course, in the purpose and the substance of the lesson—and the insight—that each text implicitly derives from the lethal accidents involved in the attempt at healing, differences the chapters in this volume seek to elucidate.

But the most peculiarly significant and the most striking feature that the three male texts turn out to have in common through the different issues they engage and through their diversity of narratives is that all of them are *stories about female resistance*. In "Adieu," the beloved woman, Stéphanie, by virtue of her madness, resists her "woman's duty"—*resists male recognition*, in unwittingly refusing to ground specularity as meaning, to serve as a narcissistic mirror for her lover and thereby to reflect back simply and unproblematically man's value. In "The Girl with the Golden Eyes," the desired woman, Paquita, by virtue of the fact that she loves a woman and that she has *two* lovers or two sexual masters, ironically and paradoxically *resists sexual appropriation*. In Freud's dream narrative the female patient, Irma, resists Freud's male "solution"; the feminine complaint *resists interpretation*; the female knot of pain resists and undercuts the mastery—and the integrity—of psychoanalytic theory.[5]

The three texts thus enact female resistance, even as they struggle with it and attempt to overcome and erase it. My strategy as reader is to encroach precisely on the female resistance in the text.

By picking up on the resistance in the text I do not propose, however, to become a "resisting reader" in the sense defined by Judith Fetterly: "Clearly, then, the first act of the feminist reader must be to become a resisting rather than an assenting reader and, by this refusal to assent, to begin the process of exorcizing the male mind that has been implanted in us."[6]

Reading and Resistance

I do indeed endorse the necessity—and the commitment—to "exorcize the male mind that has been implanted in us." But *from where* should we exorcize this male mind, if we ourselves are possessed by it, if as educated products of our culture we have unwittingly been trained to "read literature as men"—to identify, that is, with the dominating, male-centered perspective of the masculine protagonist, which always takes itself—misleadingly—to be a measure of the universal? How should we come, in other words, in possession of our female mind as distinct from the male mind into which we have been coerced? Fetterley believes that we should do the exorcizing from outside of literature, as though our feminist convictions guaranteed an immediately graspable female mind outside of culture from which to demystify the literary myths. "Such questioning and exposure," she writes, "can be carried on only by a consciousness radically different from the one that informs the literature. *Such a closed system cannot be opened up from within but only from without*" (xx; my emphasis). It is thus by stepping *outside of* literature that, in Fetterley's conception, one becomes a "resisting reader." Quoting Adrienne Rich's powerful words suggesting that rereading or "revision—the act of looking back, of seeing with fresh eyes, of entering an old text from a new critical direction—is for women more than a chapter in cultural history: it is an act of survival."[7] Fetterley concludes: "We must learn to re-read. Thus, I see my book as a self-defense survival manual for the woman reader" (vii).

But can *reading* be truly subsumed by *self-defense?* If reading has historically been a tool of revolutions and of liberation, is it not rather because, constitutively, reading is a rather risky business whose outcome and full consequences can never be known in advance? Does not reading involve one risk that, precisely, cannot be resisted: that of finding in the text something one does not expect? The danger with becoming a "resisting reader" is that we end up, in effect, *resisting reading*. But resisting reading for the sake of holding on to our ideologies and preconceptions (be they chauvinist or feminist) is what we tend to do in any case. Simply stepping outside literature by becoming a "resisting reader" might not suffice, thus, to debrief us of our "male minds."

If reading cannot be subsumed by self-defense, literature in turn cannot simply be subsumed by the cultural prejudices that traverse it and by the ideologies its authors hold. All great texts, I will propose, are literary to the precise extent that they are self-transgressive with respect to the conscious ideologies that inform them.[8] This is why my effort in this book, in being careful never to foreclose or to determine in advance the reading process, is to train myself to *tune into the forms of resistance present in the text,* those forms that make up the textual dynamic as a field of clashing and heterogeneous forces and as a never quite predictable potential of *surprise.* My effort is, in other words, not to "resist" the text from the outside but rather to seek to trace within each text *its own resistance to itself,* its own specific literary, inadvertent *textual transgression of its male assumptions and prescriptions.* Although this literary excess, this self-transgression of the text (which is, I argue, precisely what makes it a work of art: a work that no agenda can contain) might be at first invisible, inaudible, because it exceeds both the control and the deliberate intention of the writer's consciousness, I am suggesting that it can be amplified, made patent, by the desire—and by the rhetorical interposition—of a woman reader. It is this double practical process of amplification and rhetorical interposition—and its incalculable theoretical and emotional effects—which I would like here to propose.

An Ethics of Interpretation, or the Priority of Practice

The chapters that follow are my own attempts in the apprenticeship—and the enactment—of such a method, through the exploitation of different theoretical perspectives (mainly those developed in France since the 1960s) and through the concrete utilization of different resources of theory, which I reclaim from my position as a woman reader in bringing them to bear on the elaboration—and the reinvention—of new (feminist) strategies of reading. Chapter 2 (on encountering Balzac's "Adieu") practices primarily "deconstructive" and other philosophical techniques of reading (inspired mainly by Jacques Derrida and Michel Foucault)[9] for its voicing (its reclaiming) of the woman question in the text. Chapter 3 (on encountering Balzac's "The Girl with the Golden Eyes") implicates, for its interpretive illumination of the "feminine resistance" in the text, a Lacanian psychoanalytic grasp of the complexity of the manifestations of desire and of the multiplicity of levels on which human action operates and has effects—effects of difference: the imaginary, the symbolic, and the real.[10] Chapter 4 (on encountering Freud's *Interpretation of Dreams*) uses biographical, autobiographical, and Freudian psychoanalytical tools of analysis: it is informed simultaneously and differently by Freud the interpreter (the analyst, the theorist) and by Freud the dreamer (an analysand, an unconscious actor). Systematically decentered from its exclusive male enunciation through the rhetorical interposition of my own utterance, psychoanalysis is here staged—and exploited—in its double aspect as theory and as practice, as a *conceptual framework* that breaks new ground and yet, at the same time, as an idiosyncratic *clinical event* (advent), a symptomatic narrative, a process of concrete unfolding of particular discoveries and insights evolving from the difficulties of a singular life story.

All the chapters of this book are also crucially inspired, in the very heart of their endeavor, by the feminist renewal of both the theoretical and the critical perspectives, and each chapter takes its point of departure from some relevant feminist works, which it discusses. But the present book is not in any way intended as a summary, a survey, or an overview of feminist theory and scholarship. Rather, it attempts to think out new procedures of approach, to listen in new ways to both psychoanalytical and literary texts. It opens up new ways of reading as concrete events (unique encounters with another's story) and as pragmatic acts, or interventions in the process of rethinking and of modifying (personal and social) expectations.

In insisting on the origin of the present volume not in theory per se but in the production of a practice, this book encounters feminism as an enabling inspiration, not as a theoretical orthodoxy or as an authorizing new institutionalization. My endeavor is thus situated in the realm of the question Michel de Certeau has pointed to as "the antinomy" between what he defines as "ethics" and what, "for lack of a better term," he calls "dogmatism":

> Ethics is articulated through *effective operations,* and it defines a distance between what is and what ought to be. This distance designates a space where we have *something to do.* On the other hand, dogmatism is authorized by a reality it claims to represent and in the name of this reality, it imposes laws.[11]

In its dogmatic aspect, every theory is legislating. It dictates on the one hand and censors on the other. Practice is not censoring but merely showing *what can be done,* and done otherwise, for instance in the classroom, for instance with students who might very well be eager, as they often are, to acquire psychoanalytic tools of insight or to communicate with literature as some form of artistic wisdom about life. Practice does not institute its laws but shows us ways (that work or do not work: ways whose measure is not rightness but effectiveness) enabling us, as Adrienne Rich has put it, "not to pass on a tradition but to break its hold over us"[12]—enabling us, that is (I would add), to intervene in the transmission of canonic culture not just in demystifying its blind spots, its bigotry, and its coercive structures but in illuminating, at the same time, its self-critical perspectives and its own implicit (inadvertent) self-subversive insights.

Rather than attempting a dogmatic summary of feminist theory and scholarship as yet another legislating process of codification of the real and another institutional legitimation and authorization, the chapters that follow experiment pragmatically with *strategies for reading sexual difference* insofar as it specifically *eludes* codification and resists *any* legitimizing institutionalization. Each chapter explores a different strategy not merely through the use of different tools of theory but through the concrete complexity and the interpretive intensity unpredictably derived, each time, from the incomparable uniqueness of a practical textual experience. Each chapter will thereby engage, in its own way, in a reading practice whose effectiveness is coextensive with the freshness of its impact of surprise and whose endeavor is to elaborate, each time, a reading model that would be, precisely, unanticipated, different from the one imagined by the previous chapters and thus different, unanticipated, also, from one chapter to another.

II

Writing and Self-Resistance

To understand is always an ascending movement; that is why comprehension ought always to be concrete (one is never got out of the cave, one comes out of it).

—SIMONE WEIL, *First and Last Notebooks*

I did not know, however, at the outset, that such a methodology was to become the focus of my attempt; I practiced it intuitively, without at first articulating its significance. Nor did I anticipate, in the beginning, the actual (practical and theoretical) outcome of my readings. I have discovered it in process, in the course of my own readings, and more clearly, upon rereading them, upon reflecting retrospectively on their common features and their common meanings. Mainly, I did not foresee what I now term "the feminine resistance in the text," and still less could I anticipate that *all* the texts, whose authors happen to be men, that I have randomly selected for a study of the female figure would lead consistently to this common denominator, would all intersect and encounter one another on this unanticipated point of female resistance.[13]

This point has, moreover, *resisted me* for a long time; this book has been long in the making, and its writing process—not coincidentally, I would suggest—has spun out over many years. Once reclaimed, the question, "What does a woman want?" has turned out to resist closure, to inhibit my own writing, and to delay completion of this book. But it has thus exemplified ironically and vitally, in practice, at once the desire and the difficulty, or the *self-resistance*, not simply of reading as a woman (since what this means is not immediately graspable outside of the prescriptions and beliefs of patriarchal structure) but of *assuming* one's own sexual difference in the very act of reading; of assuming, that is, not the false security of an "identity" or a substantial definition (however nonconformist or divergent) but the very insecurity of a differential movement, which no ideology can fix and of which no institutional affiliation can redeem the radical anxiety, in the performance of an act that constantly—deliberately or unwittingly—*enacts* our difference yet finally escapes our own control.

"For a long time I have hesitated to write a book on woman," writes Simone de Beauvoir, introducing thus through a *self-resistance*—through this written "hesitation" built into the very move to assume her sexual difference—nothing less than the groundbreaking theory of *The Second Sex:*

> For a long time I have hesitated to write a book on woman. The subject is irritating, especially for women; and it is not new. . . . After all, is there a problem? And if so, what is it? *Are there women, really?* . . .We are extorted to be women, remain women, become women. It would appear, then, that every female human being is not necessarily a woman; to be so considered she must share in that mysterious and threatened reality known as femininity. . . .

> A man would never get the notion of writing a book on the peculiar situation of the human male. But *if I wish to define myself, I must first of all say: "I am a woman"*; on this truth must be based all further discussion.[14]

In a dialogue with Simone de Beauvoir thirty-three years after the publication of *The Second Sex*,[15] Jean-Paul Sartre reflects on the singular speech act accomplished by the book:

> *JPS:* What strikes me is that you began [*The Second Sex*] with no preconceived ideas. It wasn't a refusal or a condemnation. You

wanted to know what it meant to be a woman, probably you wanted to find out also for yourself, because you were thinking already of doing your memoirs?

SdB: Absolutely. When I started writing—it wasn't exactly memoirs, but an essay on myself—I realized that I needed first of all to situate myself as a woman. So first I studied what it meant to be a woman in the eyes of others, and that's why I talked about the myths of woman as seen by men; then I realized it was necessary to go deeper to the heart of reality, and that is why I studied physiology, history, and the evolution of the feminine condition.

JPS: It's rather odd. You began as a non-feminist, as a woman in this sense like any other woman that would have simply liked to know what it meant to be a woman. And in writing this book you became a feminist. You recognized your enemies and attacked them, and you specified what being a woman was like. This is the value of the book.

SdB: I wrote on a theoretical level. The book can be of value to feminist militants because there are not so many theorists among them, but I myself remained then on the theoretical level. It was not yet a feminist commitment such as I've been involved with in recent years.

JPS: Perhaps it's normal. It's the best way. *You became a feminist in writing this book.*

SdB: It's normal. . . . *But I became a feminist especially after the book was read, and started to exist for other women.* [Emphasis mine.]

On Becoming

The Second Sex is thus engendered by an impulse and a quest that the writing process carries out but that the author does not at first own. The book en-genders its own readers, who resonate at once to its content and to the process of its writing—that of finding out about oneself something one is not a priori in possession of, of finding out, that is, what one does not know one is or has in effect become. But it is the readers who in turn en-gender the author's knowledge of herself: "I became a feminist," says Simone de Beauvoir, "especially after the book was read and started to exist for other women." Feminism comes to be defined here almost inadvertently, as a bond of reading: a bond of reading that engenders, in some ways, the writer—leads to her full assumption of her sexual difference; a bond of reading and of writing which, however, paradoxically *precedes* knowing what it means to "read as a woman," since this very bond, this very reading, is precisely constituted by the recognition that the question "what *is* a woman?" has not yet been answered and defies, in fact, all given answers. "Are there women, really?" *The Second Sex* asks provocatively:

> One wonders if women still exist, if they will always exist, whether or not it is desirable that they should, what place they occupy in this world, what their place should be. (vii)

"One is not born, one *becomes*, a woman," writes Simone de Beauvoir (2:267). "You *became* a feminist by writing this book," says Jean-Paul Sartre. "I *became* a feminist when the book was read and started to exist for other women," says Simone de Beauvoir. The bond of reading constitutes a renewed relation to one's gender insofar as it establishes a relationship among all these becomings. *Becoming* a feminist is undertaking to investigate what it means to *be* a woman and discovering that one *is* not a woman but rather *becomes* (somewhat interminably) a woman; discovering, through others' reading and through the way in which other women are *addressed* by one's own writing, that one is not born a woman, one has become (perhaps never quite sufficiently) a woman.

If the present volume is, therefore, an inquiry into the act of reading, and specifically into what "reading as a woman" means, it is only insofar as the practical readings that compose this book encompass and unwittingly reveal the implicit story—and the autobiographical itinerary—of how one becomes a feminist. At the outset of the writing process of the book, my current feminist positions were not a given. They were neither altogether conscious nor truly owned by me with their full critical potential: I arrived at them through reading, acquired them in writing. The impact of these insights on the audiences that first heard them presented in lectures, the knowledge that early published versions of them found resonance and repercussions in female colleagues who were discussing them in conferences and assigning them in classrooms, and the letters I received from women readers in turn deepened their own impact on me and rendered more compelling and more articulate the critical significance of the feminist convictions to which the readings and the writing led me. Only much later did I realize that these readings and this writing, which kept speaking to me through their unexpected power of address and of reverberation but which at the time seemed purely theoretical and purely literary, were also coping inadvertently—although with no awareness on my part—with the reading and the writing of my own life.

III

Reading Autobiographically

Feminism, I will thus suggest, is indeed for women, among other things, reading literature and theory with their own life—a life, however, that is not entirely in their conscious possession. If, as Adrienne Rich acutely points out, rereading or "re-vision—the act of looking back, of seeing with fresh eyes, of entering an old text from a new critical direction—is for women more than a chapter in cultural history: it is an act of survival," it is because survival is, profoundly, a form of autobiography.

Reading autobiographically is, however, an activity and a performance far more complex than the mere project—and the mere stylistic trend—of "getting personal."[16] Because as educated women we are all unwittingly possessed by "the male mind that has been implanted in us," because though women we can quite easily and surreptitiously read literature as men, we can just as easily "get personal" with a borrowed voice—and might not even know *from whom* we borrow that voice. "Getting personal" does not guarantee that the story we narrate is wholly ours or that it is narrated in our own voice. In spite of the contemporary literary fashion of feminine confessions and of the recent critical fashion of "feminist confessions," I will suggest that *none of us, as women, has as yet, precisely, an autobiography.* Trained to see ourselves as objects and to be positioned as the Other, estranged to ourselves, we have a story that by definition cannot be self-present to us, a story that, in other words, is not a story, but *must become* a story.[17] And it cannot *become* a story except through the *bond of reading,* that is, through the *story of the Other* (the story read by other women, the story of other women, the story of women told by others), insofar as this story of the Other, as *our own* autobiography, *has as yet precisely to be owned.* I will suggest that it cannot be owned by our attempting a direct access to ourselves as women ("getting personal") or by our pretending to leave culture or to step outside the text (by becoming a "resisting reader"). Rather, I will here propose that we might be able to engender, or to access, our story only indirectly—by conjugating literature, theory, and autobiography together through the act of reading and by reading, thus, into the texts of culture, at once our sexual difference and our autobiography as missing.

I should hasten to explain that by adopting the generic "we" in what I have just written ("I will suggest that none of us, as women, has as yet, precisely, an autobiography"), I am not proposing to speak in the name of women: the "we" is a rhetorical structure of address, not a claim for epistemological authority. I am speaking not *for* women, but *to* women. My utterance is meant as a *speech act,* not as a constative *representation;* it is a cognitive suggestion, an intuition, but its rhetorical force is primarily performative. The contemporary female autobiographical self-consciousness is a crucially important, innovative theoretical and critical resource, and I do not mean to underestimate or undercut its strategic value. But I do propose here to *unsettle* the very notion of autobiography, precisely insofar as we have *settled* into it (I feel) a little too impatiently and self-complacently, as though we could be sure that we already have—in culture or in life—"a room of our own."

As what follows will make clear, this book is, among other things, the account of how I made the discovery—and the experience—of my own autobiography as missing, and why this *missing* of my own autobiography appears to me today to be characteristic of the female condition. I am mainly speaking for myself. And yet I venture to propose this insight as a metaphor for the dilemmas and the problematic of autobiography for women, since the observations of my personal experience cannot invalidate it with respect to any woman I know, and since I have gained this self-understanding, once again, once indirectly, by listening to other women speak about themselves, by looking closely at the stories (which narrated, ultimately, the absence of a story or, what amounts to the same thing, the presence of too many stories) of a number of close female friends.

The autobiographical testimony of various women writers (women who are culturally worlds apart from one another) seems to confirm this insight. "My life," writes English aristocrat Vita Sackville-West in the opening paragraph of her posthumous autobiography, "[is] a deceitful country."[18] What woman's life is not a "deceitful country"—mostly to herself? "I have no recollection whatsoever of having written this," attests, in her own way, French writer Marguerite Duras in the first page of her autobiographical narrative, *La Douleur.* "I know that I have [written] it, . . . I recognize the handwriting, but I do not see myself writing this journal. . . . *La Douleur* ["Pain"] is one of the most important things of my life."[19] Duras exemplifies the possibility that women have no real memory of their autobiography, or at least that they cannot simply command autobiography by the self-conscious effort of a voluntary recall. Unlike men, who write autobiographies from memory, women's autobiography is what their memory cannot contain—or hold together as a whole—although their writing inadvertently inscribes it. To the extent that "Pain" is "one of the most important things" in Duras's life, it is, like many stories of profound pain and of traumatization, a story of (partial) amnesia, a story present in the text but whose writing cannot coincide with the writer's consciousness. Indeed, I will suggest—in line with what has recently been claimed by feminist psychiatrists and psychotherapists—that every woman's life contains, explicitly or in implicit ways, the story of a trauma.[20]

When We Dead Awaken

Because trauma cannot be simply remembered,[21] it cannot simply be "confessed": it must be testified to, in a struggle shared between a speaker and a listener to recover something the speaking subject is not—and cannot be—in possession of. Insofar as any feminine existence is in fact a traumatized existence, feminine autobiography *cannot be* a confession.[22] It can only be a testimony: to survival. And like other testimonies to survival,[23] its struggle is to testify at once to life and to the death—the dying—the survival has entailed.[24]

But how do we write our own death (our own survival) and still keep the integrity, the wholesomeness, of the narrative itself? "To me," says African American feminist Bell Hooks, "telling the story of my growing up years was intimately connected with the longing to kill the self I was without really having to die. I wanted to kill that self in writing. Once that self was gone—out of my life forever—I could more easily become the me of me."[25] Is not this violent and paradoxical predicament of "writing a woman's death" precisely part of any feminist undertaking of "writing a woman's life?" "The awakening of consciousness," writes American poet Adrienne Rich, "is not like the crossing of a frontier—one step and you are in another country." Even if the crossing of the frontier of female "sleep" or numbness—the crossings by each woman of a line of death—is shared today collectively by women, even if "it is no longer such a lonely thing to open one's eyes," the *process of awakening* cannot simply be equated with the state (the dream?) of wakefulness. Rich can cite, in sympathy, Bernard Shaw's comment on Ibsen's feminist play in 1900, "What remains to be seen as perhaps the most interesting of all imminent social developments is what will happen 'When We Dead Awaken.' "[26] But when we assume and reappropriate, as women, Ibsen's title and Shaw's comment, when we become, today, the speaking subjects and the autobiographical bearers of the sentence "When we dead awaken . . . ," the sentence is no longer simply sayable, narratable as a simple story but becomes itself, upon each utterance, an *enactment*, and a *reenactment*, of its own event (its own advent). As a *story*, "When we dead awakens . . ." is, however, bound to remain split, and indeed unfinished.

This is why I have suggested that "none of us, as women, has as yet, precisely, an autobiography," and that "we have a story that by definition cannot be self-present to us, a story that is not a story but *must become* a story." Let me illustrate this by my own example, which is also the example of this book (not merely of its statements but of its utterance, and of the process of its writing).

I have written that "we might be able to engender, or to access, our story only indirectly—by conjugating literature, theory, and autobiography together through the act of reading and by reading, thus, into the texts of culture, at once our sexual difference and our autobiography as missing."

I cannot confess to my autobiography as missing, but I can testify to it.

I cannot write my story (I am not in possession of my own autobiography), but I can read it in the Other.

I realize today—but did not know at the time of writing—that my work on Balzac's "Adieu" (chapter 2) was itself reliving an "adieu," attempting to work over and think over the violent significance in my own life of a separation from a man I loved, a rupture that (as in the story) was consummated by my own geographical departure, but whose traumatic consequences I was still apparently experiencing, even though on the surface of my life this episode, which had occurred years earlier, was overcome.

I was even less aware of my own involvement in the chapter I wrote next, some two years later (chapter 3). A core curriculum course required me to teach Balzac's "The Girl with the Golden Eyes." I remember that the textual ambiguity I was attempting to decipher was entirely baffling and astonishing to me: it took me time and labor even to understand it literally, to figure out that what the text was so elliptically narrating was the story of a triangular affair, of a woman loving both a woman and a man, and that the story's ambiguities derived, primarily, from the confusion, the misreadings, the mistakes made by (experienced by) a man (a suitor) in his difficulty—and indeed his impossibility—of grasping the situation from his male perspective: a predominant, stereotypical perspective that puts men (himself included) at the center of women's lives and that cannot conceive of femininity except as subordinate to man (himself, or else a rival who must surely in turn be male) as its only center. The protagonist, Henri, thus fails to guess that his rival is in fact a woman, and tragic consequences ensue. Henri is deluded, and his reading of the sexes and of sexual difference is ironically demystified and subverted by the text. But are we not all, in fact, the cultural progeny—and cultural hostages—of this perspective? This is why it was a text so hard to read in the beginning: its interpretation had to go against the grain of universal sexual error.

Struggling with this error, struggling with the text's deception so as to articulate its truth, I failed entirely to notice my own autobiographical implication in it. It is only today, only with hindsight, with the remoteness of perspective afforded by the distance in time, that I realize how my own life, at the time of writing, involved a similar complexity (of languages, of cultures, of relations). But at the time of writing, when I was struggling with the text both to figure out its actual (factual) narrative and to analyze its philosophical and rhetorical prowesses, I had no clue, no inkling, that this testing of the virtuosity of the interpreter had anything to do with what, on different levels and in very different ways, I was also living.

If the critical suggestion I am making in this book is that people tell their stories (which they do not know or cannot speak) through others' stories, then the very force of insight of this critical suggestion was at once borne out and actively enacted, put in motion, by the process of my writing which was *driven*, in effect, by the ways in which I was precisely missing my own implication in the texts before me.*

*To be continued in chapter 5 (Afterword).

2

Women and Madness:
The Critical Phallacy

(Balzac, "Adieu")

Silence gives the proper grace to women.

—SOPHOCLES, *Ajax*

Dalila: In argument with men a woman ever
Goes by the worse, whatever be her cause.
Samson: For want of words, no doubt, or lack of breath!

—MILTON, *Samson Agonistes*

I

Woman as Madness

Is it by chance that hysteria (significantly derived, as is well known, from the Greek word for "uterus") was originally conceived as an exclusively female complaint, as the lot and prerogative of women? And is it by chance that even today, between women and madness, sociological statistics establish a privileged relation and a definite correlation? "Women," writes Phyllis Chesler, in her book *Women and Madness,* "Women more than men, and in greater numbers than their existence in the general population would predict, are involved in 'careers' as psychiatric patients."[1] How is this sociological fact to be analyzed and interpreted? What is the nature of the relationship it implies between women and madness? Supported by extensive documentation, Phyllis Chesler proposes a confrontation between objective data and the subjective testimony of women: laced with the voices of women speaking in the first person—literary excerpts from the novels and autobiographies of women writers, and word-for-word interviews with female psychiatric patients—the book derives and disputes a "female psychology" conditioned by an oppressive and patriarchal male culture. "It is clear that for a woman to be healthy she must "adjust" to and accept the behavioral norms for her sex even though these kinds of behavior are generally regarded as less socially desirable. . . . The ethic of mental health is masculine in our culture" (68–69). "The *sine qua non* of 'feminine' identity in patriarchal society is the violation of the incest taboo, i.e. the initial and continued 'preference' for Daddy, followed by the approved falling in love and/or marrying of powerful father figures" (138). From her initial family upbringing throughout her subsequent development, the social role assigned to the woman is that of serving an image, authoritative and central, of man: a woman is first and foremost a daughter/a mother/a wife. "What we consider 'madness,' whether it appears in women or in men, is either the acting out of the devalued female role or the total or partial rejection of one's sex-role stereotype" (56).

In contrast to the critical tendency prevalent in Europe, through which a certain French circle has allied itself philosophically with the controversial indictments of the English "antipsychiatry" movement, Phyllis Chesler, although protesting in turn against psychiatry as such, in no way seeks to bestow upon madness the romanticized glamour of political protest and of social and cultural contestation: "It has never been my intention to romanticize madness, or to confuse it with political or cultural revolution" (xxiii). Depressed and terrified women are not about to seize the means of production and reproduction: quite the opposite of rebellion, madness is the impasse confronting those whom cultural conditioning has deprived of the very means of protest or self-affirmation. Far from being a form of contestation, "mental illness" is a *request for help*, a manifestation both of cultural impotence and of political castration. This socially defined help-needing and help-seeking behavior is itself part of female conditioning, ideologically inherent in the behavioral pattern and in the dependent and helpless role assigned to the woman as such.

It is not the material, social, and psychological female condition but rather the very status of womanhood in Western theoretical discourse that concerns Luce Irigaray in her book, *Speculum de l'autre femme*.[2] In contrast to Phyllis Chesler, Luce Irigaray interrogates not the empirical voice of women and their subjective testimony but the key theoretical writings of men— fundamental texts in philosophy and in psychoanalysis—which, in one way or another, involve the concept of femininity. Her study focuses on the text of Freud's (fictive) lecture entitled "On Femininity" and on the feminine metaphors in Plato's Myth of the Cave. A psychoanalyst herself, Luce Irigaray adopts the traditional feminist critique of the male-centered orientation and of the antifeminine bias in psychoanalytical theory; but her elaboration and consolidation of these classical feminist arguments is derived from the philosophical methods of thinking developed in France by Jacques Derrida and others in their attempt to work out a general critical "deconstruction" of Western metaphysics. According to Derrida's radicalization of the Nietzschean and Heideggerian critiques of traditional philosophy, Western metaphysics is based on the totalitarian principle of so-called logocentrism, that is, on the repressive predominance of "logos" over "writing," on the privileged status of the present and the consequent valorization of presence. This *presence-to-itself* of a *center* (given the name of Origin, God, Truth, Being, or Reason) centralizes the world through the authority of its self-presence and subordinates to itself, in an agonistic, hierarchical manner, all the other cognizable elements of the same epistemological (or ontological) system. Thus, the metaphysical logic of dichotomous oppositions which dominates philosophical thought (Presence/Absence, Being/Nothingness, Truth/Error, Same/Other, Identity/Difference, and so on) is, in fact, a subtle mechanism of hierarchization which assures the unique valorization of the "positive" pole (that is, of a *single* term) and, consequently, the repressive subordination of all "negativity," the mastery of difference as such. It is by thus examining the mere illusion of duality and the repressive way in which the polarity Masculine/Feminine functions in Western thought so as to privilege a unique term that Luce Irigaray proceeds to develop her critical argument. Theoretically subordinated to the concept of masculinity, the woman is viewed by the man as *his* opposite, that is to say, as *his* other, the negative of the positive, and not, in her own right, different, other, otherness itself. Throughout the Platonic metaphors that will come to dominate Western discourse and to act as a vehicle for meaning, Lucy Irigaray points out a latent design to exclude the woman from the production of speech, since the woman, and the other as such, are philosophically subjugated to the logical principle of Identity—Identity being conceived as a solely *masculine* sameness, apprehended as *male* self-presence and consciousness-to-itself. The possibility of a thought that would neither spring from nor return to this masculine Sameness is simply unthinkable. Plato's text thus establishes the repressive systemization of the logic of identity: the privilege of "oneness," of the reproduction of likeness, of the repetition of sameness, of literal meaning, analogy, symmetry, dichotomous oppositions, teleological projects.

Freud, who for the first time freed thought from a certain conception of the present and of presence to oneself, whose notions of deferred action, of the unconscious, of the death instinct, and of the repetition compulsion radically undermine the classical logic of identity, remains, nevertheless, himself a prisoner of philosophy when he determines the nature of sexual difference in function of the a priori of sameness, that is, of the male phallus. Female sexuality is thus described as an absence (of the masculine presence), as lack, incompleteness, deficiency, envy with respect to the only sexuality in which value resides. This symmetrical conception of otherness is a theoretical blindness to the woman's actual Difference, which is currently asserting itself, and asserting precisely its claim to a new kind of logic and a new type of theoretical reasoning.

A question could be raised: if "the woman" is precisely the other of any conceivable Western theoretical locus of speech, how can the woman as such be speaking in this book? Who is speaking here, and who is asserting the otherness of the woman? If, as Luce Irigaray suggests, the woman's silence, or the repression of her capacity to speak, are constitutive of philosophy and of theoretical discourse as such, from what theoretical locus is Luce Irigaray herself speaking in order to develop her own theoretical discourse about the woman's exclusion? Is she speaking the language of men, or the silence of women? Is she speaking as a woman, or *in place of* the (silent) woman, *for* the woman, *in the name of* the woman? Is it enough to *be* a woman in order to *speak as* a woman? Is "speaking as a woman" a fact determined by some biological condition or by a strategic, theoretical position, by anatomy[3] or by culture? What if "speaking as a woman" were not a simple "natural" fact, could not be taken for granted? With the increasing number of women and men alike who are currently choosing to share in the rising fortune of female misfortune, it has become all too easy to be a speaker *"for* women." But what does "speaking *for* women" imply? What is "to speak *in the name of* the woman"? What, in a general manner, does "speech in the name of" mean? Is it not a precise repetition of the oppressive gesture of *representation*, by means of which, throughout the history of logos, man has reduced the woman to the status of a silent and subordinate object, to something inherently *spoken for?* To "speak in the name of," to "speak *for*," could thus mean, once again, to appropriate and to silence. This important theoretical question about the status of its own discourse and its own "representation" of women, with which any feminist thought has to cope, is not thought out by Luce Irigaray and thus remains the blind spot of her critical undertaking.

In a sense, the difficulty involved in any feminist enterprise is illustrated by the complementarity, but also by the incompatibility, of the two feminist studies just examined: the works of Phyllis Chesler and Luce Irigaray. The interest of Chesler's book, its overwhelming persuasive power as an outstanding clinical document, lies in the fact that it *does not* speak *for* women: it lets women speak for themselves. Phyllis Chesler accomplishes thus the first symbolical step of the feminist revolution: she *gives voice* to the woman. But she can only do so in a pragmatic, empirical way. As a result, the book's theoretical contribution, although substantial, does not go beyond the classical feminist thought concerning the sociosexual victimization of women. On the other side of the coin, Irigaray's book has the merit of perceiving the problem on a theoretical level, of trying to think the feminist question through to its logical ends, reminding us that women's oppression exists not only in the material, practical organization of economic, social, medical, and political structures but also in the very foundations of logos, reasoning, and articulation—in the subtle linguistic procedures and in the logical processes through which meaning itself is produced. It is not clear, however, that statement and utterance here coincide so as to establish actual feminine difference not only on the thematic but also on the rhetorical level: although the otherness of the woman is here fully assumed as the subject of the statement, it is not certain whether that otherness can be taken for granted as positively occupying the un-thought-out, problematical locus from which the statement is being uttered.

In the current context of cultural studies and its ongoing attempt at a critical transvaluation of a whole range of cultural codes, feminism encounters the major theoretical challenge of all contemporary thought. The problem, in fact, is common to the revaluation of madness as well as to the contention of women: *how can one speak from the place of the other?* How can the woman be thought about outside of the Masculine/Feminine framework, *other* than as opposed to man, without being subordinated to a primordial masculine model? How can madness, in a similar way, be conceived outside of its dichotomous opposition to sanity, without being subjugated to reason? How can difference as such be thought out as *nonsubordinate* to identity? In other words, how can thought break away from the logic of polar oppositions?

In the light of these theoretical challenges, and in keeping with the feminist questioning of psychoanalytical and philosophical discourse, it could be instructive to examine the ideological effects of the very production of meaning in the language of literature and in its critical exegesis. I therefore propose here to undertake a reading of a text by Balzac which deals with the woman as well as with madness and to examine the way in which this text, and its portrayal of feminine madness, has been traditionally perceived and commented upon. The text—entitled "Adieu"—is a short story first published in 1830 and later included by Balzac in the volume of *Philosophical Studies* of the *Comédie humaine*.[4]

The Realistic Invisible

The story is divided into three parts. The first describes a mysterious domain into which have inadvertently wandered two lost hunters: Philippe de Sucy, a former colonel, and his friend d'Albon, a magistrate. Anxious to find out where they are, they turn to two women, the only human beings in the vicinity, but their questions meet only silence: one of the women, Geneviève, turns out to be a deaf-mute, and the other an aphasic madwoman whose entire vocabulary consists of the word *adieu*. On hearing this word, Philippe faints, recognizing in the madwoman his former mistress, Countess Stéphanie de Vandières, who had accompanied him to Russia during the Napoleonic Wars but whom he has not seen again since their separation on the banks of the Berezina River and whose trace he has ever since been unable to recover.

The second part is a flashback to the war episode. Among the collapsing masses of the retreating French army, Stéphanie and Philippe are fighting against unbearable cold, inhuman exhaustion, and debilitating hunger in the midst of the snowy plains. Philippe heroically shields Stéphanie in the hope of crossing the Berezina and of thus reaching and having her reach the safety of the other side, free from the Russian threat. But when it turns out that only two places are left on the life raft, Philippe leaves them to Stéphanie and her husband, the Count of Vandières, sacrificing himself for the latter. The Count, however, never reaches the

other side: in a violent jolt during the crossing, he is swept over-
board and killed. Stéphanie cries out to Philippe, "Adieu!": it is to
be her last lucid word before she loses her reason. For two years
thereafter, she continues to be dragged along by the army, the
plaything of wretched riffraff. Mad and cast off like an animal, she
is discovered one day after the end of the war by her uncle, an
elderly doctor, who takes her in and sees to her needs.

The third part describes the combined efforts of the two
men—the doctor having been joined by Philippe—to save and to
cure Stéphanie. Stéphanie, on seeing Philippe, fails to recognize
him: her continuous repetition of the word *adieu* implies no understanding and bears no relation to conscious memory. At the
sight of the "stranger" (Philippe), she runs away like a frightened
animal. Following the advice of the doctor, Philippe learns how
to "tame" Stéphanie by giving her sugar cubes, thus accustoming
her to his presence. Philippe still hopes that Stéphanie will some
day recognize him. Driven to despair, however, by the long wait,
Philippe decides to hasten Stéphanie's recognition of him by
subjecting her to a psychodrama designed to restore her memory:
he artificially creates a replica of the Russian plains and of the
Berezina River; using peasants disguised as soldiers, he theoretically reconstructs and replays before the madwoman's eyes the
exact scene of their wartime separation. Stéphanie is thus indeed
cured: overwhelmed, she recognizes Philippe, smiles to him, repeats once again "adieu"; but at that very instant she dies.

A current pocket edition of this amazing story (published by
Gallimard in the "Folio" collection) ensures, in two different
ways, its critical presentation: the text is preceded and followed
by pedagogical commentary—a Preface by Pierre Gascar and a
"Notice" by Philippe Berthier—which is supposed to "explain" it
and "situate" its importance. It is striking that, of the three chapters that constitute this short story—the discovery of the madwoman in the mysterious domain, the war scene, and the scene of the
cure—both commentators discuss only one: the chapter depicting the war. The main plot, which consists of the story of a
woman's madness (episodes 1 and 3), is somehow completely
neglected in favor of the subplot (episode 2), a historical narrative

whose function is to describe the events that preceded and occasioned the madness. The "explication" thus excludes two things: the madness and the woman. Viewed through the eyes of the two academic critics, "Adieu" becomes a story about the suffering of men in which the real protagonists are none but "the soldiers of the Grand Army." The Preface indeed makes a great point of praising Balzac for "the realism, unprecedented in the history of literature, with which the war is here depicted":[5] "by showing us, in "Adieu," the soldiers of the Grand Army haggard, half dead with hunger and cold, draped in rags, surging toward the pontoon bridge thrown across the Berezina, he [Balzac] deals . . . the myth of military grandeur . . . a blow whose repercussions extend well beyond the post-Napoleonic era" (10–11). This supposedly objective reading of what is called Balzac's realism in fact screens out and disguises an ideological pattern of textual amputations and cuts in which only a *third* of the text is brought to the reader's attention. "Indeed," concedes the Preface's author, "these scenes do not take up much room in . . . "Adieu," where most of the action occurs subsequent to the historic events that they symbolize. *But they suffice* to give the war its true countenance" (12). As for the author of the "Notice," he does not even seek to justify the arbitrary, disproportionate cuts underlying his "explication"—by putting forward a *truth* "which suffices": "the *true* countenance of the war." In line with the academic tradition of "selected passages," he proposes, simply and "innocently," literally to *cut up* the text, to *extract* the second chapter, and truly materialize the operation of ideological extirpation with a serene pedagogical confidence: "the second chapter, *which can be isolated from the work* as was the story of Goguelat from the *Country Doctor* (cf. our edition of this novel in Folio), marks the appearance in Balzac's work of the theme of the wartime disappearance of an officer who comes back many years later" (266). The story is here explicitly summed up as being exclusively that of a man: that of "the wartime disappearance of *an officer* who comes back many years later." It is, therefore, by no means surprising to see the author of the "Notice" taken aback by the fact—to him incomprehensible—that in its second version this text could have been, as he puts it, "oddly entitled" "A Woman's Duty" (265). Evident in an abandoned title, but in the text neither seen nor heard, the woman does not belong to the realm of the "explicable"; her claim to commentary is solely an inexplicable piece of knowledge, an unusable article of erudition.

It is just in this manner that the institution of literary criticism pronounces its expert, professional discourse, without even noticing the conspicuousness of its flagrant misogyny. To the *sociological* sexism of the educational system corresponds, in this case, the naive, though by no means innocent, sexism of the exegetical system of *literary analysis*, of the academic and pedagogical fabrication of "literary" and critical discourse. By guiding the reader, through the extirpation of "explicable" facts, to the "correct" perception, to the literal "proper," so-called objective level of textual interpretation, academic criticism conditions the very norms of "legibility." Madness and women, however, turn out to be the two outcasts of the establishment of readability. An ideological conditioning of literary and critical discourse, a political orientation of reading, thus affirms itself, not so much through the negative treatment of women as through their total neglect, their pure and simple omission. This critical oversight, which appears as a systematic blindness to significant facts, functions as a censorship mechanism, as a symbolic eradication of women from the world of literature. It is therefore essential to examine the theoretical presuppositions that permit and sanction this kind of blindness.

We have seen that what is invoked so as to authorize the arbitrariness of the curtailment of the text is the critical concept of Balzac's "realism": the realism of war, "unprecedented"—as the Preface puts it—"in the history of literature." In the context of this manly realism, the woman is relegated to non-existence, since she is said to partake of the "unreal": "Beside the Berezina . . . Stéphanie's carriage, blocked among hordes of French soldiers savage with hunger and shock, becomes the *unwonted, almost unreal element* in which the whole absurdity of the situation bursts out" (11–12). What, then, is this "realism" the critic here ascribes to Balzac if not the assumption, not shared by the text, that what happens to men is more important, or more "real," than what happens to women? A subtle boundary line, which gives itself as a "natural frontier," is thus traced, in the critical vocabulary, between the realm of the "real" and that of the "unreal," between the category of "realism" and that of the so-called supernatural:

> While "Colonel Chabert" contains no *supernatural* elements, . . . "Adieu" allots a great deal of space to psychic phenomena, with Stéphanie's madness, and even to parapsychic phenomena, with her death. . . . It is noteworthy . . . that Balzac's short stories . . . devote infinitely more space to the *supernatural*, to the presence of the *invisible* . . . than do his novels. . . . In these four stories where it exists side by side with the most striking *realism, the marvellous* is in fact only represented by the *state of semi-unreality* which the main characters attain through the horror of their ordeal. We here come across . . . the romantic conception of the transfiguring power of suffering. (14–17)

The "supernatural," as everyone knows, cannot be rationally explained and hence should not detain us and does not call for thought. Flattened out and banalized into the "edifying conclusion" (17) of the beneficent power of suffering, Stéphanie's madness is not problematic, does not deserve to detain us, since it is but a "state of semi-unreality." Realism thus postulates a conception of "nature" and of "reality" which seeks to establish itself, tautologically, as "natural" and as "real." Nothing, indeed, is less neutral than this apparent neutrality; nothing is less "natural" than this frontier that is supposed to separate "the real" from "the unreal" and which in fact delimits only the inside and the outside of an ideological circle: an inside that is *inclusive* of "reason" and men, "reality" and "nature"; and an outside that is *exclusive* of madness and women, that is, the "supernatural" and the "unreal." And since the supernatural is linked, as the critic would have it, to "the presence of the invisible" (16), it comes as no surprise to find the woman predestined to be, precisely, *the realistic invisible*, that which realism as such is inherently unable to see.

It is the whole field of a problematic, which defines and structures the invisible as its definite outside—excluded from the domain of visibility and defined as excluded by the existence and the structure of the problematic field itself. . . . The invisible is defined by the visible as *its* invisible, its prohibited sight. . . . To see this invisible . . . requires something quite different from a sharp or attentive eye, it takes an *educated eye*, a revised, renewed way of looking, itself produced by the effect of a "change of terrain" reflected back upon the act of seeing.[6]

With a "revised" way of looking, "educated" by the "change of terrain" brought about by the feminist interrogation, let us now attempt to reread Balzac's text and to reinterpret its relation to the woman as well as to madness.

II

"She? Who?"

From the very beginning the woman in this text stands out as a problem. The opening pages present the reader with a series of abstract questions concerning a female identity: the two lost hunters are trying to situate themselves, to ascertain the identity of the woman they have just glimpsed in the unknown place into which they have wandered: "Where the devil are we?" "She, who?" "Where are we? What is that house? Whose is it? Who are you? Do you live here?" "But who is this lady?" "She? Who?"[7]

As readers we, too, cannot get our bearings: deluged with questions, at the same time deprived systematically of information, not really knowing *who* is speaking, much less about whom, we are in turn as lost in the text as the two protagonists are in geographical space. The text thus originates in the *loss* of the very conditions of localization and identification, in a general state of confusion from which, in an almost anonymous manner, a recurrent question emerges: "She? Who?" The feminine pronoun preceding any proper denomination, the ambiguous question preceding any informative clarification, this preliminary inquiry takes on an abstractly emphatic and allegorical character and seems to situate from the start the textual problematic within a systematic search for the nature of feminine identity. From the beginning, however, the question reaches a dead end: addressed to the women themselves, the query meets only silence, since both women here are deprived of the ability to speak. Addressed to others, the question obtains only distant and hypothetical answers: "But who is this lady?" "It is presumed that she comes from Moulins . . . ; she is said to be mad. . . . I wouldn't guarantee you the truth of these rumours" (164).

The allegorical question, "She? Who?" will thus remain unanswered. The text, nonetheless, will play out the question to its logical end, so as to show in what way it *precludes* any answer, in what way the question is set as a trap. The very lack of the answer will then write itself as a different question, through which the original question will find itself dislocated, radically shifted and transformed.

"She? Who?" The women cannot respond: mad, they do not understand the men's questions. Nor do the rational men understand the senseless words of the women. But the women, though mad, understand each other. The doctor thus interprets the friendship that seems to unite Stéphanie and the peasant Geneviève: "Here . . . she has found another creature she seems to get along with. It's an idiot peasant woman. . . . My niece and this poor girl are in a way united by the invisible chain of their common destiny, and by the feeling that causes their madness" (196). Understanding occurs in this text only on one side or the other of the boundary line that, separating silence from speech, distinguishes madness from reason. It is nonetheless striking that the dichotomy Reason/Madness, as well as Speech/Silence, exactly coincides in this text with the dichotomy Men/Women. Women as such are associated both with madness and with silence, whereas men are identified with the prerogatives of discourse and of reason. In fact, men appear not only as the possessors, but also as the dispensers, of reason, which they can at will mete out to—or take away from—others. While Philippe and the doctor undertake to "restore Stéphanie's reason," the magistrate, on the other hand, brags: "If you should ever bring a suit to court, *I would make you lose it, even if reason were a hundred percent on your side*" (150). The three men in the story in fact symbolically represent—by virtue of their professions: magistrate, doctor, soldier—the power to act upon others' reason, in the name of the law, of health, or of force.

With respect to the woman's madness, man's reason reacts by trying to appropriate it: in the first place, by claiming to "understand" it, but with an external understanding that reduces the madwoman to a spectacle, to an *object* that can be known and possessed. "Go on, Sir, leave her alone," the doctor recommends to Philippe. "I know how to live with the dear little creature; I *understand* her madness, I *spy upon* her gestures, I am in on her secrets" (208–9). To "spy on" in order to "know"; to "tame" in order to "cure": such are the methods used by masculine reason so as to *objectify* feminine madness, and thereby to master it. If the madwoman is throughout the story seen as and compared to an animal, this pervasive metaphor tells us less about Stéphanie's delirium than about the logic of her therapists. For the object is precisely to capture the animal and to tame it. Thus we see the symbolic import of the initial hunting scene. A metaphorical parody of the episode of war and of its martial logic (" 'Come on, deputy, forward! Double time! Speed up. . . . March over the ruts. . . . Come on, march! . . . If you sit down, you're lost' " [147, 151], the opening scene of the hunt already symbolically prefigures Philippe's attitude toward Stéphanie: "Come on," cries Philippe from the very first, not yet knowing whom he is talking about but integrating as a matter of course the woman into his hunter's mentality, "Come on, let's run after the white and black lady! Forward!" (157). But the hunter's chase will here be but the measure of the flight of his prey.

If masculine reason thus constitutes a scheme to capture and master, indeed, metaphorically *rape* the woman, by the same token, Stéphanie's madness is not contingent on but directly related to her femininity: consisting, precisely, in its loss. Several times Philippe, in fact, explicitly defines Stéphanie's madness as the loss of her womanhood. When the doctor advises him to tame her by feeding her pieces of sugar, Philippe sadly answers: "*When she was a woman*, she had no taste for sweets" (202). And again, in a burst of sorrow, Philippe cries: "I die a little more every day, every minute! My love is too great! I could bear everything if only, in her madness, she had kept some *semblance of femininity*" (208). Madness, in other words, is precisely what makes a woman *not* a woman. But what is a "woman"? Woman is a "name," denied in fact to Geneviève in the same way as it is denied to Stéphanie: "Then a *woman*, if such a *name* can be applied to the *undefinable being* who got up from under the bushes, pulled on the cow by its rope" (159). "Woman" is consequently a "definable being"— chained to a "definition" itself implying a model, a definition commanded by a *logic of resemblance*. Even in the war scene, Stéphanie had already lost her "femininity" "[when] all rolled around herself, *she really resembled nothing. . . .* Was this that *charming woman, the glory of her lover, the queen of the Parisian ballrooms?* Alas! even the eyes of her most devoted friend could perceive *nothing feminine* left in that heap of linens and rags" (180). If a "woman" is strictly, exactly, " what *resembles* a woman" ("she really resembled nothing . . . nothing feminine left"), it becomes apparent that "femininity" is much less a "natural" category than a rhetorical one, analogical and metaphorical: a metaphorical category that is explicitly bound, as perceived by Philippe, to a sociosexual stereotype, to the "definable" role of the mistress—"the queen of the Parisian ballrooms." Of course, the "queen" here implies a king; the literal, *proper* meaning of metaphorical femininity, paradoxically enough, turns out to be a masculine property: the "queen of the Parisian ballrooms," "that charming woman," is above all, *"the glory of her lover."* "Woman," in other words, is the exact metaphorical measure of the narcissism of man.

The Masculine thus turns out to be the universal equivalent of the opposition: Masculine/Feminine. It is insofar as Masculinity conditions Femininity as its universal equivalent, as what determines and measures its value, that the textual paradox can be created according to which the woman is "madness," while at the same time "madness" is the very "absence of womanhood." The woman is "madness" to the extent that she is other, *different* from man. But "madness" is the "absence of womanhood" to the extent that "womanhood" is what precisely *resembles* the Masculine universal equivalent, in the polar division of sexual roles. If so, the woman is "madness" since the woman is *difference;* but "madness" is "nonwoman" since madness is the *lack of resemblance.* What the narcissistic economy of the Masculine universal equivalent tries to eliminate, under the label "madness," is nothing other than *feminine difference.*

III

The Therapeutic Fallacy

Such is the male narcissistic principle on which the system of reason, with its therapeutic ambition, is based. For, to "restore Stéphanie's reason" signifies, precisely, to reinstate her "femininity": to make her recognize man, the "lover" whose "glory" she ought to be. "I'm going to the Bons-Hommes," says Philippe, "to see her, speak to her, *cure* her. . . . Do you think the poor woman would be able to *hear me* and *not recover her reason?*" (197). In Philippe's mind, "to recover her reason" becomes synonymous with "to hear *me.*" "The cure of the madman," writes Michel Foucault, "is in the reason of the other—his own reason being but the very truth of his madness."[8] Stéphanie's cure is in Philippe's reason. The "recovery" of her reason must thus necessarily entail an act of recognition:

> "She doesn't recognize me," cried the colonel in despair. "Stéphanie! It's Philippe, your Philippe, Philippe!" ("Adieu," 200–201)

> "Her; not to recognize me, and to run away from me," repeated the colonel. (201)

> "My love," he said, ardently kissing the countess's hands, "I am Philippe." "Come," he added, . . . "Philippe is not dead, he is here, you are sitting on his lap. You are my Stéphanie, and I am your Philippe." "Adieu," she said, "adieu." (207)

Stéphanie's recovery of her "reason," the restoration of her femininity as well as of her identity, depends then, in Philippe's eyes, on her specular recognition of *him*, on her *reflection* of his own name and of his own identity. If the question of female identity remains in the text unanswered, it is simply because it is never truly asked: in the guise of asking, "She? Who?" Philippe is in fact always asking, "I? Who?"—a false question, the answer to which he believes he knows in advance: "It's Philippe." The question concerning the woman is thereby transformed into the question of a guarantee for men, a question through which nothing is questioned, whose sole function is to ensure the validity of its predefined answer: "You are *my* Stéphanie." The use of the possessive adjective makes explicit the act of appropriation focused here on the proper names. But it is from Stéphanie's own mouth that Philippe must obtain his proper name, his guarantee of the propriety of his own identity, and of hers: Stéphanie = Philippe, "You are my Stéphanie, and I am your Philippe." In Philippe's eyes, Stéphanie is viewed above all as an object whose role is to ensure, by an interplay of reflections, his own self-sufficiency as a "subject," to serve as a mediator in his own specular relationship with himself. What Philippe pursues in the woman is not a face but a mirror, which, reflecting his image, will thereby acknowledge his narcissistic self-image. "Women," writes Virginia Woolf, "have served all these centuries as looking-glasses possessing the magic and delicious power of reflecting the figure of man at twice its natural size." Philippe, as it turns out, desires not *knowledge* of Stéphanie herself but her *acknowledgment* of him: his therapeutic design is to restore her not to *cognition*, but to *recognition*.

To this demand for recognition and for the restoration of identity through language, through the authority of proper names, Stéphanie opposes, in the figure of her madness, the dislocation of any transitive, communicative language, of "propriety" as such, of any correspondence or transparency joining "names" to "things," the blind opacity of a lost signifier unmatched by any signified, the pure recurrent difference of a word detached from both its meaning and its context.

"Adieu," she said in a soft harmonious voice, but whose melody, impatiently perceived by the expectant hunters, seemed to divulge not the slightest feeling or the least idea. (163)

"Adieu, adieu, adieu!" she said, without her soul's conferring any perceptible inflection upon the word. (200)

To this automatic repetition of senselessness and difference, Philippe in turn will oppose another type of repetition designed precisely to restore resemblance and identity: in order to cure Stéphanie, in order to restore to her demented, dislocated language its nominative and communicative function, he decides to reproduce the primal scene of the "adieu" and thus to re-present theatrically the errant signifier's lost significance, its proper signified. Without her knowledge, Stéphanie will literally be forced to play herself, to return to her "proper" role. Through the theatrical setup, everything will end up making sense: and, with all difference thus erased, re-presentation necessarily will bring about the desired re-cognition.

The baron [de Sucy] had, inspired by a dream, conceived a plan to restore the countess's reason. . . . He devoted the rest of the autumn to the preparation of this immense enterprise. A small river flowed through his park where, in the winter, it flooded an extensive marsh that resembled . . . the one running along the right bank of the Berezina. The village of Satou, set on a hill, added the final touch to put this scene of horror in its frame. . . . The colonel gathered a troop of workers to dig a canal that would represent the voracious river. . . . Thus aided by his memory, Philippe succeeded in copying in his park the riverbank where General Elbe had built his bridges. . . . The colonel assembled pieces of debris similar to what his fellow sufferers had used to construct their raft. He ravaged his park, in an effort to complete the illusion on which he pinned his last hopes. . . . In short, he had forgotten nothing that could reproduce the most horrible of all scenes, and he reached his goal. Toward the beginning of December, when the snow had blanketed the earth with a white coat, he recognized the Berezina. This false Russia was of such appalling truth that several of his comrades recognized the scene of their former sufferings.

Monsieur de Sucy kept the secret of this tragic representation.
(209–10)

The cure succeeds. However, so as to fulfill perfectly her
"Woman's Duty," to play her role correctly in this theater of the
identical, to recognize specularly and reflect perfectly Philippe's
"identity," Stéphanie herself must disappear: she has to *die* as
other, as a "subject" in her own right. The tragic outcome of the
story is inevitable, inscribed as it is from the outset in the very
logic of representation inherent in the therapeutic project. Stéphanie will die; Philippe will subsequently commit suicide. If, as
ambiguous as it is, the cure turns out to be a murder, this murder,
in its narcissistic dialectic, is necessarily suicidal,[9] since, killing
Stéphanie in the very enterprise of "saving" her,[10] it is also his
own image that Philippe strikes in the mirror.

Through this paradoxical and disconcerting ending, the text
subverts and dislocates the logic of representation that it has
dramatized through Philippe's endeavor and his failure. Literature thus breaks away from pure representation: when transparency and meaning, "reason" and "re-presentation" are regained,
when madness ends, so does the text itself. Literature, in this way,
seems to indicate its impuissance to dominate or to recuperate the
madness of the signifier from which it speaks, its radical incapacity to master its own signifying repetition, to "tame" its own
linguistic difference, to "represent" identity or truth. Like madness and unlike representation, literature can signify but not *make
sense.*

Once again, it is amazing to what extent academic criticism,
completely unaware of the text's irony, can remain blind to what
the text says about itself. It is quite striking to observe to what
extent the logic of the unsuspecting "realistic" critic can reproduce, one after the other, all of Philippe's delusions, which the
text deconstructs and puts in question. Like Philippe, the "realistic" critic seeks representation, tries, by means of fiction, to reproduce "the real thing," to reconstruct, minutely and ex-
haustively, the exact historical Berezina scene. Like Philippe, the
"realistic" critic is haunted by an obsession with proper names—

identity and reference—sharing the same nostalgia for a transparent, transitive, communicative language, in which everything possesses, unequivocally, a single meaning that can be consequently mastered and made clear, in which each name "represents" a thing, in which each signifier, properly and adequately, corresponds both to a signified and to a referent. On the critical as well as on the literary stage, the same attempt is played out to appropriate the signifier and to reduce its differential repetition; we see the same endeavor to do away with difference, the same policing of identities, the same design of mastery, of *sense control.* For the "realistic" critic, as for Philippe, the readable is designed as a stimulus not for knowledge and cognition but for acknowledgment and *re-cognition*, not for the *production* of a question, but for the *reproduction* of a foreknown answer—delimited within a preexisting, predefined horizon, where the "truth" to be discovered is reduced to the natural status of a simple given, immediately perceptible, directly "representable" through the totally intelligible medium of transparent language. Exactly in the same way as Philippe, the commentators of "Adieu" are in turn taken in by the illusory security of a specularly structured act of recognition. Balzac's text, which applies as much to the "realistic" critic as to Philippe, can itself be read as a kind of preface to its own Preface, as an ironic reading of its own academic reading.

For, what Philippe *misrecognizes* in his "realistic" recognition of the Berezina is, paradoxically enough, the *real:* the real not as a convergence of reflections, as an effect of mirroring focalization, but as a radically decentering resistance; the real as, precisely, other, the unrepresentable as such, the eccentric residue that the specular relationship of vision cannot embrace.

Along with the illusions of Philippe, the "realistic" critic thus repeats, in turn, his allegorical act of murder, his obliteration of the other: the critic also, in his own way, *kills the woman*, while killing, at the same time, the question of the text and the text as a question.

But here again, as in Philippe's case, the murder is incorporated in an enterprise that can be seen as "therapeutic." For in obliterating difference, in erasing from the text the disconcerting and eccentric features of a woman's madness, the critic seeks to "normalize" the text, to banish and eradicate all trace of violence and anguish, of scandal or insanity, making the text a reassuring, closed retreat whose balance no upheaval can upset, where no convulsion is of any consequence. "To drive these phantoms firmly back into their epoch, to close it upon them, by means of a historical narrative, this seems to have been the writer's intent."[11] By reducing the story to a recognition scheme, familiar, snug and canny, the critic, like Philippe, "cures" the text, precisely of that which in it is incurably and radically uncanny.

From this paradoxical encounter between literature's critical irony and the uncritical naivety of its critics, from this confrontation in which Balzac's text itself seems to be an ironic reading of its own future reading, the question arises: how *should* we read? How can a reading lead to something other than recognition, "normalization," and "cure"? How can the critical project, in other words, be detached from the therapeutic projection?

This crucial theoretical question, which undermines the foundations of traditional thought and whose importance the feminist writings have helped to bring out, pinpoints at the same time the difficulty of the woman's position in today's critical discourse. If, in our culture, the woman is by definition associated with madness, her problem is how to break out of this (cultural) imposition of madness *without* taking up the critical and therapeutic positions of reason: how to avoid speaking both as *mad* and as *not mad*. The challenge facing the woman today is nothing less than to "reinvent" language, to *re-learn how to speak:* to speak not only against, but outside of the specular phallocentric structure, to establish a discourse the status of which would no longer be defined by the phallacy of masculine meaning. An old saying would thereby be given new life: today more than ever, changing our minds—changing *the* mind—is a woman's prerogative.

3

Textuality and the Riddle of Bisexuality

(Balzac, "The Girl with the Golden Eyes")

> Rereading, an operation contrary to the commercial and ideological habits of our society, which would have us "throw away" the story once it has been consumed . . . so that we can then move on to another story, buy another book . . . , rereading is here suggested at the outset, for it alone saves the text from repetition (those who fail to reread are obliged to read the same story everywhere).
>
> —ROLAND BARTHES

"The Riddle of Femininity"

"Today's lecture," wrote Freud in 1932, "may serve to give you an example of a detailed piece of analytic work, and I can say two things to recommend it. It brings forward nothing but observed facts . . . , and it deals with a subject which has a claim on your interest second almost to no other":

> Throughout history people have knocked their heads against the riddle of the nature of femininity. . . . Nor will *you* have escaped worrying over this problem—those of you who are men; to those of you who are women this will not apply—you are yourselves the problem.[1]

Intended for "an audience gathered from all the Faculties of the University,"[2] the lecture, entitled "Femininity," was in fact never delivered. Having undergone an operation for mouth cancer, its author was no longer in a condition to deliver public lectures. And thus he wrote, prefacing his own unspoken lecture:

> A surgical operation had made speaking in public impossible for me. If, therefore, I once more *take my place in the lecture room* during the remarks that follow, it is only by an artifice of the imagination; it may help me not to forget to *bear the reader in mind* as I enter more deeply into my subject.[3]

I would here like to take my place as reader—as a reader of "Femininity" and as a reader of femininity—by reflecting, first, on its relation to Freud's place: to Freud's place in the lecture room, at once real and imaginary, of the University of Vienna; the place he addresses and from which he asks the question of femininity. In quoting Freud's introductory remarks as an introduction to this essay—itself originally delivered as a public talk—I have displaced, however, the locus of the question to another lecture room and to another structure of address. Thus, when I said along with Freud, "Today's lecture . . . has a claim on your interest second almost to no other," and, "I can say two things to recommend it," "today" was not 1932 but 1989; the "you" addressed was not the Viennese university public but a contemporary American audience gathered for a feminist colloquium; and my usage of the first person *I* introduced into the quotation a discrepancy of genders, since Freud's *I* implied the male gender, whereas I addressed the public as a woman. Consequently, when I then went on to quote, "throughout history men have knocked their heads against the riddle of femininity. . . . Nor will *you* have escaped worrying over this question— those of you who are men; to those of you who are women this will not apply—" the audience—as I had expected—did not fail to laugh.

What are the implications of this laughter? It was brought about by an awareness—at once spontaneous and historical—of the spatial, temporal, and sexual displacement that my enunciation operated in Freud's statement. But this historical aware-ness—the discrepancy named "history" which my reading intro-duced into Freud's text as a difference from itself—only made apparent the inherent textual discrepancy between Freud's *state-ment*, opening up the question *of* the Woman, and his *utterance*, closing it *for* women, excluding women from the question: "to those of you who are women, this will not apply—you are your-selves the problem."

"Those of you who are men," on the other hand, will not "have escaped worrying over this problem." A question, Freud thus implies, is always a question of desire; it springs out of a desire that is also the desire for a question. Women, however, are con-sidered merely as the *objects* of desire, and as the *objects* of the question. To the extent that women "*are* the question," they cannot *enunciate* the question; they cannot be the speaking *subjects* of the knowledge or the science that the question seeks.

In assuming here my place as a speaking subject, I have then *interfered*, through female utterance and reading, in Freud's male writing. I have *enacted* sexual difference in the very act of reading Freud's interrogation of it; enacted it as precisely difference, with the purpose not of rejecting Freud's interrogation, but of displac-ing it, of carrying it beyond its *stated* question, by disrupting the transparency and misleadingly self-evident universality of its male enunciation.

Freud, indeed, in spite of his otherwise radical approach, still articulates "the riddle of femininity" in typical nineteenth-century terms. His question: "What is femininity?" in reality asks: "What is femininity—*for men?*" My simple (female) reitera-tion of Freud's question—with the rhetorical effect of the public's laughter—has somewhat redefined the "riddle" and implied a slightly different question: What does the question, "What is femininity—*for men?*" mean *for women?*

It is this question that I propose to address in the present chapter, through a reading of an ingenious text by Balzac which, in its turn, dramatizes the "riddle of femininity" as the double question of the reading of sexual difference and of the interven-tion of sexual difference in the very act of reading.

I

"Gold and Pleasure": Social Classes and Sex Roles

The text in question, Balzac's short novel entitled "The Girl with the Golden Eyes,"[4] is in fact literally a provocative erotic *riddle*, specifically addressing the question of sexual difference: dramatizing, in a triangular complication, the interferences of an affair between a man and a woman with an existing affair between two women, depicting both the interplay and the conflict between homosexual and heterosexual loves, the text at once explores and puts in question the very structure of opposition between the sexes, as well as the respective definitions of masculinity and femininity.

The erotical narrative, however, is preceded by a long discursive preamble in which the narrator depicts a panoramic analytical picture of Paris and its social classes. The classes are separated, economically distinguished, according to their material wealth, according to the amount of gold that they possess or do not possess; but they are also united by their common desire for "gold" and for "pleasure": the self-destructive drive for ever-increasing amounts of money and enjoyment canalizes the social energies on all class levels. Paris is thus viewed by Balzac as a battlefield of interests and passions in which "everything stimulates the upward march of money" (318), each "sphere" throwing its "spawn into a superior one," each class endeavoring to rise to a higher social rank, in order "to obey that universal master, gold or pleasure" (316, TM). "Who . . . is dominant in this country. . . ? Gold and pleasure. Take these two words as a light," says Balzac (310–11, TM).

What is then the connection, the question arises, between Balzac's "light" and Balzac's darkness, between this discursive sociological treatise on Parisian society and the rather obscure erotical narrative that follows? How does the *class struggle* depicted in the prologue relate to the *sex struggle* around which the story revolves?

It would seem, at first sight, that what is common to the two struggles is the very structure of *division* from which they spring, as well as the principle of *hierarchy*, which in both cases organizes the division as an authoritative order. The prologue's hierarchical division of social classes would thus correspond to the story's hierarchical division of sexual roles, according to which, in Balzac's society as well as in ours, the female occupies the inferior position, whereas the male, in much the same way as the class possessing the gold, occupies the superior, ruling position.

It is no coincidence that the feminine heroine, Paquita, is a slave whose origin is "a country where women are not human beings, but chattels. One does what one likes with them, sells them, buys them, kills them. In fact one uses them to indulge one's whims, just as here you make use of your furniture" (390). The alibi of a foreign country's cultural manners should not, however, mislead us, since it is in Paris that Paquita is thus disposed of, being sexually used and unscrupulously murdered. It is equally in Paris that Henri de Marsay pronounces his contemptuous verdict on women:

> And what then is woman? a little thing, a bunch of twaddle. With two words spoken in the air, can't she be made to work for four hours? She is sure that the fop will take care of her, because he does not think of great things. . . . Indeed, a fop cannot help being a fop if he has a reason for being one. It's the women who give us this rank. The fop is the colonel of love, he is a lady killer, he has his regiment of women to command. . . . So therefore foppishness . . . is the sign of an unquestionable power conquered over the female population. (348–49, TM)

It is in these terms, by this verdict on women, that Henri de Marsay defines his own foppishness as well as his male role in the story, the typical male role of the Parisian civilization. According to these well-defined masculine/feminine social roles, the relationship between man and woman is one of sexual hierarchization, in which the man is the master, whereas the woman is reduced to the state of a mere slave, at once man's pleasure object and his narcissistic assurance of his own importance, value, and power.

Gold and Femininity

This culturally determined male attitude can also, more subtly, be analyzed, not through Henri's contempt for "the female population" of Paris but through his admiration for an exceptional woman—the girl with the golden eyes—whose desirable image strikes him as his feminine ideal, the very incarnation of the woman of his dreams:

> Last Thursday . . . I was strolling about . . . , I found myself face to face with a woman. . . . This was no case of stupefaction, nor was she a common streetwalker. Judging from the expression on her face, she seemed to be saying: "What! you are here, my ideal, the being I have thought of, dreamed of night and morning! . . . Take me, I am yours. . . ." And so on. . . . So I looked at her closely. My dear fellow, from a physical standpoint, this incognita is *the most adorably feminine woman I have ever met. . . . And what most struck me straightaway,* what I still find fascinating, is *her two eyes,* yellow as a tiger's; yellow as *gleaming gold; living gold, brooding gold, amorous gold, gold that wants to come into your pocket. . . .* Ever since I have taken interest in women, my unknown *she* is the only one whose virginal bosom, whose ardent and voluptuous curves have realized for me the unique woman of my dreams. . . . *She is the very essence of woman,* an abyss of pleasures whose depths may never be sounded: *the ideal woman.* (337–39, TM, emphasis mine)

Clearly Henri is here attracted to the girl's golden eyes because they are for him the sign of feminine desire and sexuality, the very incarnation of femininity per se. However, what are the connotations of the metaphor of gold that, through her eyes, comes to symbolize the girl and, thus, to embody ideal femininity? By virtue of its very brilliance, the "gleaming gold" ("*jaune d'or qui brille*") is essentially a *reflective* substance, which reflects a source of light external to itself; the light reflected comes indeed from the object contemplated by the woman— Henri himself: the golden eyes of femininity are fundamentally a *mirror* in which the male—Henri—can contemplate his own idealized self-image so as to admire himself: "Judging from the expression on her face, she seemed to be saying: 'What! you are here, my ideal, the being I have thought of, I have dreamed of night and morning!' " (338).

The golden brilliance of the girl with the golden eyes is fascinating, says Henri, because it is an "amorous gold, gold that wants to come into your pocket." Paradoxically, gold as the metaphor of the utmost value is an image, at the same time, of *possession* and *appropriation*, through which the ideal woman is again reduced to a mere *object*, whose sole function is to be possessed and owned by man. But the metaphor evoked by Henri of the gold that wants to come into his pocket is even more ambiguous than that, since, carrying a clear erotic connotation suggestive of the sexual act, it grants the golden eyes of femininity a phantasmic masculine—phallic—role. Ironically enough, femininity itself thus turns out to be a metaphor of the phallus. To the extent that the girl with the golden eyes is here viewed by Henri as the tool for his purely narcissistic satisfaction, Henri's desire for the ideal woman can be said to be a sort of masturbation fantasy: his own phallus is indeed the prize he seeks. In much the same way as, in the prologue, gold was said to be the ruling principle, a principle of domination and of hierarchy, so the golden phallus in the story, beckoning from behind the mask of woman's beauty, is to be wishfully recuperated and restored to its proper place: man's pocket.

The girl with the golden eyes is thus the very name of woman and of femininity *as a fantasy of man*. The name, indeed, was given to the girl by a group of men—Henri's friends. Defined by man, the conventional polarity of masculine and feminine names woman as a *metaphor of man*. Sexuality, in other words, functions here as the sign of a rhetorical convention, of which woman is the *signifier* and man the *signified*. Man alone has thus the privilege of proper meaning, of *literal* identity: femininity, as signifier, cannot signify *itself*; it is but a metaphor, a figurative substitute; it can but refer to man, to the phallus, as its proper meaning, as its signified. The rhetorical hierarchization of the very opposition between the sexes is then such that woman's *difference* is suppressed, being totally subsumed by the reference of the feminine to masculine identity.

II

A Question of Address

When Henri decides to possess, that is, to place in his pocket, the gold of the girl with the golden eyes, he has first to find out who she is. Having followed the girl to the house where she lives, he charges his valet to spy on the mailman and shrewdly extort from him the name of the target of his desire. In order to ward off the mailman's suspicion, the valet is furnished with a false package, which he supposedly has to deliver to the golden-eyed girl. Having learned from the mailman that the house belongs to Don Hijos, Marquis de San Réal, the valet mistakenly concludes that the woman desired by his master must be the marquis's wife. "My package," he thus tells the mailman, "is for the Marquise" (342). But he soon realizes his mistake when the mailman, responding to a bribe offer, informs him of the presence of still another woman in the Marquis's house. The mailman then shows him the address on a letter he has to deliver: the real name of the golden-eyed girl is Paquita Valdès. On the basis of this information, the valet, and Henri in his turn, will make a second mistake, assuming that Paquita must then be the mistress of the marquis. The drama of desire being a triangular one, the marquis, Henri mistakenly thinks, must therefore be his rival and his enemy.

> The report made by his valet Laurent had enormously enhanced the value of the girl with the golden eyes. Battle had to be given to some secret antagonist, as dangerous, it seemed, as he was cunning. To gain the victory all the forces at Henri's command would not be superfluous. He was about to act the eternally old, eternally new comedy with three characters: an old man, Don Hijos, a girl, Paquita, and a suitor, de Marsay. (347)

If Henri's story seems, at its outset, to follow indeed the conventional triangular pattern of erotic competition, of rivalry in desire, the seemingly banal triangle is an uncanny one to the extent that Henri has no real knowledge, in fact, of his partners in the triangle. Engaged as he is in the very act of desiring and of struggling, of opposing, Henri does not really know who it is that he truly desires, who it is that he truly opposes, who are the two other poles of the triangle that implicates him and structures his own sexual involvement. The episode with the mailman, more crucial than it appears to be, outlines thus the basic unconscious inquiry that governs Henri's adventure: the question is indeed one of *addresses*. Through his valet, Henri asks the mailman: what is the real address of the message of my desire? Whom do I really desire? For whom, in fact, is my package? And what, on the other hand, is the true address (the true addressee) of my hostility, of my aggressivity? Who is my real enemy? These two basic questions, pertaining to the address of desire and to the identity of the enemy, immediately translate themselves into two *interpretative mistakes*: "My package is for the marquise," says Laurent; the enemy is the marquis, thinks Henri. Whereas the first mistaken assumption is quickly dispelled and corrected, the second mistake is there to stay, in Henri's interpretation as well as in that of the reader, until the dénouement of the story, in which Henri, along with the reader, discovers that Henri's rival is not the *marquis* but the *marquise*. The mistake, in other words, consists in the substitution of the *masculine* for the *feminine*. It is therefore governed by the logic of the rhetorical hierarchy of the polarity masculine/feminine, according to which the signified (i.e., meaning) is as such necessarily *masculine*, can only be read in the masculine. But the story on the contrary shows this rhetorical presupposition to be indeed an ironic error. Henri, as well as the reader, has to learn, as the text puts it, to "read this page, so brilliant in its effect, and guess its hidden meaning" (376, TM). If Henri's drama springs from a *misreading of femininity*, consisting in a blind substitution of the masculine for the feminine, what Henri has to learn is precisely how to read femininity; how to stop reading through the exclusive blind reference to a masculine signified, to phallocentric meaning.

The Sex of Reading

The substitution, by Henri, of the masculine for the feminine in his attempt to read the proper name of his enemy, is by no means the only error in the story. Ironically enough, Paquita commits a strikingly similar, although diametrically opposed, mistake. In much the same way as Henri—a typical ideological product of the ruling male civilization—is unable to read in the feminine, Paquita, by reason of the coercive and restrictive education to which she has been subjected, is unable to read in the masculine. Having been confined as a slave since the age of twelve in sexual bondage to the marquise, Paquita—in the most literal manner— does not know what a man is, before her encounter with Henri. That is why her understanding of the opposition masculine/ feminine takes the feminine as its point of reference. When she sees Henri for the first time, she is struck by his resemblance to the *woman* she knows and loves—the marquise—who, we will later learn, is really Henri's sister. "It's the same voice," said Paquita in a melancholy tone, "and the same ardent passion" (361). Paquita then falls in love with Henri because of his very resemblance to the woman she knows. In their first sexual scene, Paquita makes Henri dress as a woman, so that he might better resemble the original model, the feminine referent: a wish that Henri unsuspectingly obeys as a pure fantasy. Paquita's very innocence thus becomes an ironic reversal of the conventional functioning of the polarity masculine/feminine: like the feminine for Henri, the masculine for Paquita signifies not itself but its symmetrical, specular opposite. The feminine is at first for Paquita the *proper meaning* of the masculine. Whereas Henri's ideal woman is a metaphor of the phallus, Paquita's ideal man is a metaphor of a woman.[5]

Since Paquita makes Henri wear a woman's dress, Henri, unwittingly, becomes a transvestite. Balzac's text could be viewed, indeed, as a rhetorical dramatization and a philosophical reflection on the constitutive relationship between transvestism and sexuality, that is, on the constitutive relationship between sex roles and clothing. If it is clothes, the text seems to suggest, if it is clothes alone, that is, a cultural sign, an institution, which determine our reading of the sexes, which determine masculine and feminine and insure sexual opposition as an orderly, hierarchical polarity; if indeed clothes make the *man*—or the woman—are not sex roles as such, inherently, but travesties? Are not sex roles but travesties of the ambiguous complexity of real sexuality, of real sexual difference? Paquita's ideal man is but a travesty of feminine identity, in much the same way as Henri's ideal woman is a travesty of masculine identity. Henri's masculine sex role for Paquita and Paquita's feminine sex role for Henri are thus but transvestisms of the other sex's deceptively unequivocal identity; that is, they are travesties of a travesty.

If transvestism then refers sexuality to clothes, to the cultural institution of the sign, travesty is possible because signs function not just grammatically, according to a norm, but rhetorically, through substitutions. Transvestism is indeed an arbitrary sign whose signifier is displaced onto a signified not "its own," an exiled signifier that no longer has, in fact, a "proper" signified, a "proper" meaning, a claim to literality. Transvestism, in Balzac's story, links sexuality to rhetoric, and rhetoric to sexuality: "*Tu travestis les mots*" ("You disguise—you travesty—your words" (377), says Henri to his friend Paul de Manerville, unwittingly suggesting that transvestism as well as travesty are conditioned by the functioning of language; that sexes can be substituted, that masculine and feminine can be exchanged, or travestied, because words can be.

Active Discretion

Henri, indeed, exposes a whole theory of rhetoric relating sexuality to language through two principles of "discretion":

> When you find yourself in need of discretion, learn this: there are *two kinds, one active, one negative. Negative discretion* belongs to the dolts who have recourse to *silence, denial,* frowning faces, the discretion which takes effect behind closed doors—sheer impotence! *Active discretion proceeds by blunt assertion.* (375, emphasis mine)

Active discretion, in other words, consists not in denying what one wants to hide, nor in simply keeping silent about it but in positively saying something else, in making a concrete erotic *affirmation* altogether different, so as to displace the focus of attention, to divert suspicion from the fact to be concealed. Of active discretion, Henri says, "The best kind of discretion . . . consists of compromising a woman we're not keen on, or one we don't love or don't possess, in order to preserve the honor of the one we love sufficiently to respect her. The former is what I call the *screen-woman*" (375, TM). The rhetoric of sexuality is thus a rhetoric of screens: of what Henri calls "negative discretion"— euphemisms and understatements—or of what he calls positive, "active discretion," the ostentatious use—in a kind of erotic overstatement—of a *screen-woman*.

The question here arises: if a woman can as such be but a screen, what can she screen? Is there, in Balzac's text, a screen-woman? Who is she? Where are the screens? And what is being screened? Can the polarity of masculine and feminine itself be modified, affected by the screen procedure, by the subversive power of linguistic travesty, by the potentiality of transvestism built into language?

A screen can have a triple function: it can serve to divide or separate, to conceal or hide, to protect or shield. In a sense, it could be said that the marquise, Henri's sister, is the screen-woman, since she literally tries to screen Paquita—to hide Paquita from the world and to hide the world from Paquita. In so acting, she constitutes a screen between Paquita and Henri. Henri's attempt, of course, is to break through, to traverse that screen. But the marquise inadvertently reemerges as a screen—as a barrier— between the lovers when Paquita, by mistake, cries out her name at the very height of her ecstatic sexual intercourse with Henri.

> At the very moment when de Marsay was forgetting everything and was minded to take possession of this creature for ever, in the very midst of ecstasy a dagger-stroke was dealt him which pierced his heart through and through: the first mortification it had ever

received. Paquita, who had found strength enough to lift him above her as if to gaze upon him, had exclaimed: "Oh! Mariquita!"

"Mariquita!" the young man roared out. "Now I know all that I didn't want to believe." (383–84)

Paquita's exclamation was the more hateful to him because he had been hurled down from the sweetest triumph which had ever exalted his masculine vanity. (385)

Paquita's exclamation is a double insult to Henri, and a symbolic emasculation, first, because the name she calls out in her ecstasy is not his own, and second, because not only is he a mere substitute, but he is obviously being substituted for a *woman*. It is thus the very name Mariquita that becomes a screen between the lovers: a screen because it separates them; a screen because it is a woman's name that names a man; a screen in that it is a substitute, a *proper* name which names *improperly:* the very name, indeed, of impropriety.

The screen is thus a *signifier,* and the signifier's implications could extend beyond its simple referent, the woman it refers to. Mariquita, indeed, is not just a woman's name; it also means, in Spanish, an effeminate man; its implicit connotation of homosexuality, although obviously linked to the marquise's name as well as to her sexual mores, cannot but reflect back upon Henri, whom it renames. Furthermore, the name *Mariquita* can be read as a composite, either of *mar*quise and Pa*quita* or of *Mar*say (Hen*ri*) and Pa*quita*; as a signifier, the word *Mariquita* thus names both Paquita's ambiguity as part of two different couples and the linkage of de Marsay and Paquita in Mariquita, that is, the triangular linkage that ties together de Marsay, Paquita, and Mariquita. Paradoxically, the screen between the lovers, the name *Mariquita*, while it separates them, also metonymically links them to each other. The screen is a triangle. And the triangle is a screen in that it cancels out, precisely, the propriety of its three proper names, setting them in motion, as interchangeable, in a substitutive signifying chain that subverts, along with their propriety, their opposition to one another, subverting, by the same token, the clear-cut polarity, the symmetrical, dual opposition, of male and female, masculine and feminine.

III

Effects of Impropriety

No longer pointing to opposed "*proper* places," to literal referential poles, but to successive *roles* in a triangular, dynamic spatial figure, to respectively opposed but interchangeable positions in a structure that subverts propriety and literality, the polarity of masculine and feminine itself becomes dynamic and reversible. However, the substitutions of woman for man and of man for woman, the interchangeability and the reversibility of masculine and feminine manifests a discord that subverts the limits and compromises the coherence of each of the two principles.

The male-centered cultural division of sex roles, the hierarchical model of male domination that conventionally structures the relationship of man and woman, through which Henri indeed expects to dominate Paquita, is thereby equally subverted or unsettled, since the master-slave relation of male to female presupposes the transparent, unified identity of each, and particularly, the coherent, unequivocal *self-identity* of the ruling male. This male self-identity, however, and the mastery to which it makes a claim, turns out to be a sexual as well as a political fantasy, subverted by the dynamics of bisexuality and by the rhetorical reversibility of masculine and feminine. If Paquita is indeed a slave, she nonetheless undermines Henri's delusion that he is her master when it turns out that she has still another master. But the marquise is not Paquita's real master either, since her hierarchical claim as Paquita's owner is equally frustrated by Paquita's love affair with Henri. If both Henri and the marquise treat Paquita as an object (be it a precious object—gold—to be owned and guarded in one's pocket), Paquita usurps the status of a subject from the moment that she takes *two lovers*—has two masters. The golden eyes of ideal femininity thus turn out to be deceptive:

having two lovers, subject to a double visual fascination and infatuation, the mirroring, brilliant golden vision no longer reflects the idealized *unified* self-image of the lover but his *division*, his fragmentation. The golden eyes do not keep their phantasmic promise: the gold is not to be possessed; all it does is *disown* the marquise and *dispossess* Henri of the illusion of his self-identical master-masculinity. The signifier "femininity" no longer fits in the code of male representation or in any representative unequivocal code; it is no longer representative of the signified masculinity, nor is it any longer representative of *any* single signified. It is precisely constituted in *ambiguity*, it signifies itself in the uncanny space *between two signs*, *between* the institutions of masculinity and femininity. It is thus not only the conventional authority of sovereign masculinity that Paquita's femininity threatens, but the authority of any representative code as such, the smooth functioning of the very institution of representation.

The Secret Enemy

It is this threat that Henri plots to eliminate through Paquita's murder: the physical suppression of Paquita's life, repressing femininity as difference, as otherness, would eliminate ambiguity as such, stabilize the suddenly drifting cultural signs, insure the principle of hierarchy and of representation, reestablish the univocality of the political institution of sexuality, that is, of culture.

It is, however, once again the marquise who precedes Henri and kills Paquita. Henri arrives at the murder scene only to find the dagger—an obvious phallic symbol—already thrust into Paquita's chest; the masculine sign of power has once again been usurped by a woman. "Ah!" de Marsay cried. . . . "This woman will even have robbed me of my revenge!" (387). In the very moment of his attempt to deny, through an act of violence, woman's power, Henri finds himself in the dénouement, once again, face to face with its castrating image. But most uncannily, this terrifying image has suddenly become his own.

Faced with the spectacle that offered itself to his eyes, Henri had more than one cause for astonishment. The marquise was a woman. . . . The girl with the golden eyes lay dying. . . . The marquise was still holding her blood-stained dagger. . . . The marquise was about to fling herself on the divan, . . . stricken with despair. . . . This movement enabled her to notice Henri de Marsay.

"Who are you?" she said, rushing upon him with raised dagger.

Henri seized her by the arm, and thus they were able to look at each other face to face. A shocking surprise chilled the blood in the veins of both of them and they stood trembling like a pair of startled horses. In truth, the two Menaechmi could not have been more alike. In one breath they asked the same question: "Is not Lord Dudley your father?"

Each of them gave an affirmative nod.

"She remained true to the blood line," said Henri, pointing to Paquita.

"She was as free of guilt as it is possible to be," replied Margarita-Euphemia-Porraberil, throwing herself on Paquita's body with a cry of despair. (388–90, TM)

This recognition scene finally provides the answer to the question that has obsessed Henri throughout the story: who is the secret enemy? What is the identity of the rival, of the third term in the triangular drama of desire? But the answer, at last revealed and clarified, is by no means a simple one, since Henri's enemy is his duplicate in every sense: in this uncanny mirror game of doubles over the corpse of their mutual victim, Henri beholds in his enemy the exact reflection of his own desire and of his own murderous jealousy; the enemy has his own voice, his own face; the enemy, in other words, is *himself.* The recognition scene thus meets and illustrates, in a striking, unexpected manner, Freud's psychoanalytic definition of the "uncanny" (*das Unheimliche*) as the anxiety provoked through the encounter with something that, paradoxically, is experienced as at once foreign and familiar, distant and close, totally estranged, unknown, and at the same time strangely recognizable and known. What, indeed, could be more distant from oneself, more foreign and estranged, than one's very enemy? What, on the other hand, is closer to oneself than oneself? But Balzac's text, in much the same way as Freud's text, postulates the meeting of extremes. The enemy—the embodiment of foreignness and distance—here uncannily turns out to be the very image of familiarity and closeness.

> "We will meet again," said Henri. . . .
>   "No, brother," she said. "We shall never meet again. I shall return to Spain and enter the convent of Los Dolores."
>   "You are too young and beautiful for that," said Henri, taking her in his arms and kissing her. (391)

What could be suspected in the recognition scene, and becomes apparent in these lines, is the connotation of incestuous desire between the brother and the sister. Narcissistic incest is indeed the implied logical consequence of the narcissistic structure of their mutual desire for Paquita; it is the secret figure that, throughout the novel, this particular triangle geometrically builds up to: since Paquita's golden eyes are but a mediating mirror in which the brother and the sister, each in his turn, behold their own idealized self-images, fall in love with their own reflections, it is but natural that they would equally desire *their own image* in each other, each being an exact *reflection* of the other.

The Purloined Package

What the dénouement reveals, then, is that, paradoxically enough, it has been Paquita—the apparent female center of the story—who has in fact all along been the *screen-woman*, screening an incestuous (unconscious) narcissistic fantasy. The golden eyes themselves were thus the screen: the screen has been a mirror, blinding in its refractions, dazzling in its bright intensity, screening through its very golden brilliance and its play of ray deflections and reflections. It is therefore through Paquita's murder—through the physical annihilation of the screen—that the face-to-face encounter between the brother and the sister is made possible.

In this manner, the dénouement provides a second unexpected answer to the second question outlined by the story: what is the true *address* of Henri's desire? Looking back again at the initial scene in which Henri's valet interrogates the mailman in the hope of finding out the true address of Henri's false package, the name of the desired woman, the true address, in other words, of Henri's message of desire, we can now fully understand the dramatic irony and symbolic impact of the valet's mistake, in saying: "My package is for the marquise." For as it turns out, Henri's package is, indeed, unwittingly, *for the marquise.* Let it be recalled, in this conjunction, that the mailman shows the valet Paquita's name and address on the envelope of a letter sent from London, sent—as we will later gather—by the marquise. Symbolically, it is therefore from the start the marquise who *gives* Henri the *address* of his desire; and indeed, materially and literally, Paquita's address and the address of the marquise are the same. Furthermore: the phonetic resonance of the name Paquita resembles the phonetic resonance of the French word *paquet*, "package." In much the same way as the true address of Henri's message of desire is mediated by the false package, Paquita herself, as the screen-woman, turns out to be but a false package whose function ultimately is to be eliminated, having brought together brother and sister, the addressor and his real addressee. Paquita, in other words, can be said to be, ironically, Henri's uncanny *purloined package.*

IV

The Father's Name

The narrative's completion of the suggestive figure of incestuous desire brings back to the text the forgotten father figure of Lord Dudley. This rhetorical return of the father, both doubled and materialized by the actual return of the marquise from England, the father's country, illustrates again Freud's definition of the uncanny as a return of the repressed, as the recurrence of "something familiar and old-established in the mind that has been estranged only by the process of repression."[6] Lord Dudley has indeed *rhetorically* been repressed at the beginning of the story, where he is mentioned, as it were, for the last time, as *that of which the text will speak no more:*

> But *let us finish with Lord Dudley* [Lord Dudley, *pour n'en plus parler*]: he came and took refuge in Paris in 1816 in order to escape from English justice, which gives its protection to nothing exotic except merchandise [qui, de l'Orient, ne protège que la marchandise]. The itinerant lord saw Henri one day and asked who the beautiful young man was. On hearing his name, he said: "Ah! He's my son. What a pity!" (331)

This euphemistic passage seems to point to Lord Dudley's homosexuality: Dudley must have fled to Paris to escape prosecution for his homosexual mores, euphemistically referred to as an Oriental import outlawed by the English courts. Lord Dudley's cynical understatement, "He's my son. What a pity!" seems to imply that, having come across Henri in Paris, the father has unwittingly lusted after his own handsome son. The rhetorical return in the dénouement of the rhetorically repressed Lord Dudley thus connotes the return both of incest and of homosexuality.

But Lord Dudley, let us not forget, is equally involved with women: it is indeed his unwanted, multiplied, and disseminated fatherhood that accounts for the story: "To make this story comprehensible, we must at this point add that Lord Dudley naturally found many women ready enough to strike a few copies of so delightful a portrait. His second masterpiece of this kind was a girl called Euphémie. . . . Lord Dudley gave his children no information about the relationships he was creating for them here, there, and everywhere" (331). If, therefore, in the recognition scene between the brother and the sister, the father's name suddenly emerges in the very place of the erased name of the girl with the golden eyes, it is not just because both names evoke bisexuality, but because they both occupy a symmetrical place in two symmetrical triangles: in much the same way as Paquita, having two love affairs, occupies the midposition between her first love and her second, between Euphémie and Henri, Lord Dudley, in the primal scene triangle, occupies the midposition between his first love affair, Henri's mother, and his other love affair, Euphé-

mie's mother, and consequently also between Henri and Euphé-
mie. Furthermore, being a foreigner in Paris, as is the father,
Paquita can only speak to Henri and communicate with him in
English: his father tongue.

Occupying thus the same position in the symbolic structure,
Paquita's gold ultimately comes to symbolize the father. The
signifier *gold* is itself inscribed in the father's name: the French
pronunciation of the word *Lord* (lor') would phonetically resemble, be in fact a homonym of, the word *l'or* (gold). The desired
golden eyes turn out to be, indeed, the family jewels. And just as in
Paquita's case, the golden eyes themselves ultimately constitute a
screen, so in the father's case it is gold that *screens* the *father's
name*, which conceals the fatherhood, since it is gold that buys the
"artificial" father, the parental substitute, de Marsay, who, for the
money he is paid by Dudley, accepts to act as father, to recognize
Henri as his son and give Henri his name.

The return of the lost *name of the father* in the dénouement
therefore strips Henri of his (adoptive) proper name, de Marsay,
leaving him, indeed, with *no name* that he can claim to be *his own*,
that he can claim to be his *proper* name. The cultural procedure of
name giving as insuring representative authority is no longer
valid in the story: the (male) authority of name givers, custom-
arily father and husband, is here disrupted: the father is no longer
truly and legitimately *represented* by the son, in much the same
way as the masculine is no longer truly and legitimately represented by the feminine. The Name of the Father, which traditionally is supposed to symbolize and to guarantee both propriety
(proper name) and property (gold), turns out to symbolize
both *impropriety*, loss of proper name, and *dispossession*, loss of
gold: it emerges in the very place of the symbolic loss of the
golden eyes.

Gold and Meaning, or the Paternity of the Prologue

Gold itself, the very fetish of desire, the very principle the prologue establishes as that which makes society go round, no longer

incarnates the economic principle of *property* and of possession but rather the economic principle of *substitution* and replacement, the very principle of endless circulation of screening substitutes and their blind fetishization.

It is because the fetish is a screen, the very screen of substitution, the screen of screening, that Henri, so as to join the girl with the golden eyes, had to agree to be blindfolded, and that he has symbolically to lose the golden eyes so as to face the gold inscribed—as signifier, not as signified—in the father's name.

The opposition between *gold* as signified and *gold* as signifier, the displacement and disruption of the one by the other, was indeed prefigured at the outset by the *narrative's first word:* the word that serves as a *transition* between the prologue and the story. It is noteworthy and quite striking that, right after the prologue has established the word *or* ("gold") as an all-encompassing explanatory guiding "light," as the authoritative sign of meaning, the narrative is, in its turn, introduced by the word *or.* This *or,* however, is just a homonym, and not a synonym, of the prologue's "gold": since it is used as a *coordinate conjunction,* it is a signifier not of the (luminous) precious substance but of the *logical relation* between the prologue and the story, a logical relation that is by no means clear and whose meaning (although ironically articulated by the signifier *or*) can no longer be "taken as a light":

> *Or,* par une de ces belles matinées du printemps . . . , un beau jeune homme . . . se promenait dans la grande allée des Tuileries.
>
> [*Now* (thus? however?), on one of those beautiful spring mornings . . . , a handsome young man . . . was sauntering along the main avenue of the Tuileries gardens.] (327, TM)

Constituting the ambiguous *transition* between the introductory authoritative discourse and the narrative, joining the prologue's gold and the story of the girl with the golden eyes, does the signifier, the conjunction *or,* mean "thus" (logically introducing an argument in support of a thesis), or does it mean "however" (logically introducing an objection)? Through this conjunction, does the story serve to *illustrate* the prologue, as a slave would serve its master[7] (*or* = "thus"), or is the story, on the contrary, a rhetorical *subversion* of the authority (of the paternity or consciousness) of the prologue (*or* = "however")?

Narrative Insubordination

It could be said that, through the chiasmus, the reversal operated by the story's dénouement within the very import and significance of the sign "gold," the narrative indeed ends up subverting, to some extent at least, the "guiding light" of the prologue, the authoritative truth that was supposed to be its "proper" meaning and which it had to "demonstrate" as a self-evident principle of identity and value which, while distinguishing between the social classes, organizes Paris as a social universe of *order* and of ascending *hierarchy*. But in the narrative, on all three levels of the story—the level of the economical class struggle, of the political sex struggle, and of the rhetorical sense struggle—the signifier *gold* turns out to be no longer a principle of identity, of order, and of hierarchy but rather, on the contrary, a principle of universal economical *equivalence* that subverts the "proper" in every sense and thus upsets the hierarchical coherence and legitimacy of classification and of class, whether political (social classes, poor as opposed to rich), rhetorical (substitutive metaphorical as opposed to literal; figurative meaning as opposed to "proper" meaning), or sexual (female as opposed to male). The prologue can no longer be *represented* by the narrative, in much the same way as, in the story's dénouement, the father can no longer be represented by the son, or the signified "gold" by its signifier, or the signified "male" by the signifier *female*.

Difference

The principle of identity is subverted along with the principle of opposition when Henri discovers, in the recognition scene, that the Same is uncannily Other and that the Other is uncannily the

Same: what he had expected to be Other—his rival's face—is Same; what he had expected to be Same—his rival's sex—is Other. Difference, Henri thinks, is determined by sexual identity. As it turns out, identity itself is determined by sexual difference. What the uncanny mirror game of the recognition scene suddenly reveals to Henri is womanhood, not as manhood's specular reflection but as the disorienting incarnation of real sexual difference: "Faced with the spectacle which offered itself to his eyes, Henri had more than one cause for astonishment. The marquise was a woman" (388, TM). What is the significance of this final revelation of the woman to Henri, as the ultimate signifier of the story?

The incestuous desire for the feminine sisterly double can be read as a fantasy of a return to the womb, to femininity as mother, a fantasy that Freud precisely mentions in his discussion of "The Uncanny": "It often happens," writes Freud, "that male patients declare that they feel that there is something uncanny about the female":

> This *unheimlich* place, however, is the entrance to the former *heimat* [home] of all human beings, to the place where everyone dwelt once upon a time and in the beginning. There is a humorous saying, "Love is a home-sickness," and whenever a man dreams of a place or a country and says to himself, still in the dream, "this place is familiar to me, I have been there before," we may interpret the place as being his mother's . . . body. In this case, too, the *unheimlich* is what was once *heimisch*, homelike, familiar; the prefix "un" is the token of repression. (153)

Since Henri's sister is a marquise, she can equally evoke Henri's mother, who was also a marquise. Henri's entire drama within the close interiority of the boudoir of the San Réal mansion betrays a womb nostalgia, a nostalgia for the woman as a familial and familiar essence, a nostalgia for femininity as snug and canny, *heimlich*, that is, according to Freud's definition, "belonging to the *house* or to the *family*," "tame, companionable to man" (126).

Paquita, however, let us not forget, must be sacrificed, eliminated, killed, so that this incestuous return to the womb can occur. The nostalgia for *heimlich* femininity, for the woman as the tame, domesticated essence of domesticity and homeliness turns out to be a deluded, murderous narcissistic fantasy that in reality represses femininity as difference, kills the real woman.

Furthermore, the narcissistic *heimlich* union with familial and familiar femininity itself turns out to be *un*heimlich and *un*canny. For in the mirror, Henri has to recognize incarnated by his double—by his sister—his own feminine reflection: he sees *himself* as a woman. Henri uncannily thus finds himself face to face with his own castration, symbolized at once by this reflection of his woman's face and by his loss of the golden eyes, through which he could complacently behold his own idealized male self-image, his univocal masculine literality. Dethroned from the privilege of unequivocal self-present literality, the masculine can no longer signify itself with a sign of plenitude. If femininity becomes indeed a signifier of castration, it is by no means here the embodiment of *literal castration*, the literalization of the figure of castration (as it sometimes is in Freud), but rather (as I understand the most radical moments of Freud's insight—as well as of Balzac's text), castration as a differential process of substitution, subverting, on the contrary, literality as such.

Masculinity, Henri discovers, is not a substance of which femininity would be the *opposite*, that is, at once the *lack* and the negative *reflection*. Since Henri himself has a woman's face, the feminine, Henri discovers, is not *outside* the masculine, its reassuring canny *opposite*, it is *inside* the masculine, its uncanny *difference from itself*.

The Uncanny and the Woman

"What interests us most in this long extract," writes Freud in his study on "The Uncanny," after having examined the lexicological and philological implications of the term, of the word *unheimlich* as opposed to *heimlich*,

> What interests us most . . . is to find that among its different shades of meaning the word *heimlich* exhibits one which is identi-

cal with its opposite, *unheimlich*. What is *heimlich* thus comes to be *unheimlich*. . . . In general we are reminded that the word *heimlich* is not unambiguous, but belongs to two sets of ideas. . . . on the one hand, it means that which is familiar and congenial, and on the other, that which is concealed and kept out of sight. The word *unheimlich* is only used . . . as the contrary of the first signification and not of the second. (18)

Thus *heimlich* is a word the meaning of which develops towards an ambivalence, until it finally coincides with its opposite, *unheimlich*. (131)

One might say, following Freud's analysis, that what is perhaps most uncanny about the uncanny is that it is not the opposite of what is canny but, rather, that which uncannily *subverts the opposition* between "canny" and "uncanny," between "heimlich" and "unheimlich." In the same way, femininity as real otherness, in Balzac's text, is uncanny in that it is not the opposite of masculinity but *that which subverts the very opposition of masculinity and femininity*.

Masculinity is not a substance, nor is femininity its empty complement, a *heimlich* womb. Femininity is neither a metonymy, a snug container of masculinity, nor is it a metaphor—its specular reflection. Femininity *inhabits* masculinity, inhabits it as otherness, as its own *disruption*. Femininity, in other words, is a pure difference, a signifier, and so is masculinity; as signifiers, masculinity and femininity are both defined by the way they differentially relate to other differences. In "The Girl with the Golden Eyes," femininity, indeed, is rigorously *the substitutive relationship between different screens*.

The dynamic play of sexuality as *difference* in the recognition scene between the brother and the sister takes place, indeed, not only *between* man and woman, between Henri and Euphémie, but between the masculinity and femininity of each. If the girl with the golden eyes was thus a *screen* between Henri and Euphémic, her symbolic screening function was not just to screen the other woman but to be a screen between Henri and his own femininity, to travesty, disguise, or hide from Henri's eyes his own split otherness, his own division as a subject, his own castration, reassuringly projected outside of himself onto his external female partner. Paquita, in other words, was a screen to the extent that she embodied the bar of censorship that separates consciousness from the unconscious. The golden eyes therefore function precisely as the prefix *un* in *unheimlich*, a prefix that Freud defines as the very "token of repression," screening the unconscious differential energy. Paquita as the bar of censorship insures the deceptively unequivocal ideological functioning of the phantasmically reified and fetishized *institutions* of masculinity and femininity.

The Cover-Up

With Paquita's death, the golden veil is torn, the bar of censorship is for a moment lifted, Henri and Euphémie can see into their own difference from themselves, into their own constitutive division and castration; but this uncanny moment of intolerable insight and of terrifying knowledge will itself be soon repressed with the cover-up of Paquita's murder and the new linguistic screen, the final euphemism that commits the murder—and the whole adventure—to forgetfulness:

> A week later Paul de Manerville met de Marsay in the Tuileries Gardens. . . .
> "Well now, you rascal, what has become of our lovely GIRL WITH THE GOLDEN EYES?"
> "She's dead."
> "Of what?"
> "A chest ailment [*De la poitrine*]." (391)

"La poitrine," or the ailing "chest"—a euphemism for consumption—is of course a lie, a social cover-up, which at the same time euphemistically and cynically describes the truth of Paquita's death through the dagger thrust into her chest; it can also euphemistically mean that Paquita has indeed died of the heart, as a metaphor for her love; she has died of her emotional and passionate involvement with Henri. The chest, however, can also euphemistically, through a dramatic textual irony, point to a sign of female difference, a signifier of femininity. In this sense, the text could here be answering that the girl with the golden eyes has died *because she is a woman;* she was sacrificed, repressed, because she incarnated femininity as otherness, as real sexual difference.

Paquita's death is thus a rhetorical transition from "active discretion" to a passive, "negative discretion," from an erotical affirmation, from the overstatement of a screen-woman, to an erotical negation, to euphemistic understatements. It is no coincidence that Henri's sister, the woman who is revealed to Henri through Paquita's murder, through the erasure of the screen-woman, is called Euphémie, Euphemia, Euphemism.[8] Femininity is in this text at once the relationship and the difference between "positive" and "negative" discretion, between a screen-woman and a euphemism. Ultimately, femininity itself becomes a euphemism, a euphemism at once for difference and for its repression, at once for sexuality and for its blindness to itself; a euphemism for the sexuality of speaking bodies and their delusions and their dreams, determined by a signifier fraught with their castration and their death. With the novel's final euphemism, however, with Paquita's death of "a chest ailment"—*de la poitrine*—femininity becomes indeed a *euphemism of euphemism*, a figure of the silencing of the very silencing of woman, of the repression of the very functioning of repression. The text, nonetheless, through its very silencing of death by language, opens up an ironic space that articulates the force of the question of femininity as the substitutive relationship between blind language and insightful, pregnant silence—between a language threatened and traversed by silence, and the silence out of which language speaks.

4

Competing Pregnancies:
The Dream from which
Psychoanalysis Proceeds

(Freud, *The Interpretation of Dreams*)

I

Psychoanalysis and Feminism: Questions of Approach

"The greatest part of the feminist movement," writes Juliet Mitchell, "has identified Freud as the enemy":

> It is held that psychoanalysis claims women are inferior and that they can achieve true femininity only as wives and mothers. . . . I would agree that popularized Freudianism must answer to this description, but the argument of this book is that a rejection of psychoanalysis is fatal for feminism. However it may have been used, psychoanalysis is not a recommendation *for* patriarchy, but an analysis *of* one. If we are interested in understanding and challenging the oppression of women, we cannot afford to neglect it.[1]

Like Mitchell, I am concerned with the misguided feminist belief that identifies Freud as the enemy of women: I take this attitude to be a grave misreading that fundamentally misconstrues both psychoanalysis and its as yet unexplored potentialities for a feminist reflection. Like Mitchell, I believe that feminism—the struggle toward a new feminine awareness fighting sex discrimination and redefining male and female sex roles—cannot afford to disregard psychoanalysis. I also believe, however, that psychoanalysis cannot afford to disregard—as Mitchell ultimately does—the feminist critique of psychoanalysis. I agree that psychoanalysis is not a recommendation or normative prescription for, but rather an analysis of, the patriarchal symbolic system in which we live. I am not as sure, however, that *as* an analysis of patriarchy, Freudian psychoanalysis is entirely transparent to itself, entirely conscious of its full ideological implications. Thus, although I basically agree with most of the specifics of Mitchell's corrective readings of the feminist *misreadings* of psychoanalysis, and although in practice I admire and endorse Mitchell's paradoxical position as a feminist advocate of Freud, I cannot endorse, in theory, the unbreachable totality of the advocacy, that is, its implicit theoretical assumption that Freud, because he was the genius that he was, was inherently incapable of error, prejudice, or oversight: that Freud is thus by definition innocent of *any* feminist critique. To the feminist charge that Freud's views of femininity were tainted, or distorted, by the sexual ideology of his times, Mitchell answers: "As Octave Mannoni says, Freud made history, he was not made by it" (328).

Freud did make history. But does the experience of making history entirely exclude that of being made by it? Do we really have here a symmetrical alternative, a simple binary opposition of active/passive, either/or? "The setting or personality of a scientist," writes Mitchell, "by definition of his work, is largely irrelevant; if it becomes relevant, then we have to question whether it is a science that he is working in" (323). Can we be so sure that we *do not* have to put in question the particular scientific status of psychoanalysis? Freud himself, who referred to many of his theories as "his mythologies," was far less optimistic and far less apt to take for granted the scientific purity of his new method of investigation and of his innovative theoretical speculation. Perhaps a book like Mitchell's shows, indeed—because of the admirable, unflinching rigor of its psychoanalytic argument countering the feminist critique—why psychoanalysis is *not* a science: because it is, precisely, *irrefutable*. To suggest, however, that psychoanalysis is not—or may not be—a simple science, is by no means to disqualify the truth inherent in its theory or the efficiency proceeding from its practice. "Psychoanalysis," says Lacan, "has to be taken seriously, even though it is not a science. It is not a science because—as Karl Popper has amply demonstrated—it is irrefutable. It is a *practice*. . . . All the same, psychoanalysis has consequences."[2]

Beyond Reversed Polarizations

Even though I sympathize with Mitchell's paradoxical position as a feminist advocate of Freud, then, I feel the need to advocate a different kind of advocacy. I cannot, psychoanalytically speaking, endorse the totality of the defense, that is, Mitchell's total rejection of the feminist critique of Freud, in much the same way as I cannot endorse the feminist critique's total rejection of Freud's theories and texts. "What all these [feminist] writers share," writes Mitchell pertinently, "is . . . a fundamental rejection of the two crucial discoveries of psychoanalysis: the unconscious and with it infantile sexuality. . . . Of course without [these two basic psychoanalytic concepts], Freud's theories of sexual difference become far easier to attack—for then, *robbed of their entire significance*, they are only prejudices." "My concern here," Mitchell perspicaciously goes on, "is in the main with the [feminist] denial of the unconscious" (352). And yet, does not Mitchell's symmetrical reversal of the feminist critique, her absolute rejection of what this critique points to as Freudian oversights, itself partake—ironically enough—of a *denial of the unconscious*, to the extent that it implicitly assumes, in the claim it makes to Freud's total awareness and total lucidity, that Freud himself had no unconscious—no (possible, conceivable) blind spots?

An absolute loyalty to Freud's consciousness is, paradoxically enough, a disloyalty to—a denial of—his theory of the unconscious. Perhaps we cannot avoid denying the unconscious, whatever we may choose to say, and in particular in any polemical pronouncement. Perhaps every *defense* entails such a *denial*, whether the defense is that of feminism against what it takes to be the aggression of psychoanalysis on the interests of women, or (as in Mitchell's case) that of psychoanalysis against what it takes to be the aggression of the feminist critique on its theoretical integrity (in both senses of the word).

But psychoanalysis precisely teaches us that every human knowledge has its own unconscious, and that every human search is blinded by some systematic oversights of which it is not aware. This is true as well of psychoanalysis itself, which cannot except itself from its own teaching. And, of course, it is also true of feminism. The unconscious means that every insight is inhabited by its own blindness, which pervades it: you cannot simply polarize, oppose blindness and insight (whether such polarization then equates blindness with feminism and insight with psychoanalysis, or on the contrary puts the insight on the side of feminism and the blindness on the side of psychoanalytic theory). Unfortunately, Mitchell's attitude only *reverses* the polarization but does not restructure, undermine, the illusory polarities.

The need for a restructuring of the symmetrically antagonistic, polar structure that has defined (delimited and limited the possibilities of) the feminist debate, has been well seen, and quite incisively articulated, in Betty Friedan's book, *The Second Stage*.[3] While I do not necessarily endorse Friedan's political solutions nor adhere to the specifics of her choices and ideological positions, I think she masterfully points out, and analyzes, the methodological impasse that the feminist critique has reached in many areas through a stereotyping of its own polarized positions.

> The feminine mystique[4] was obsolete. . . . It was, is, awesome— that quantum jump in consciousness. A whole new literature, a new history, new dimensions in every field are now emerging, as the larger implications of women's personhood and equality are explored. The women's movement, which started with personal truth not seen or understood by the experts, or even by the women

themselves, has, in the span of one generation, changed life, and the accepted image. (31)

Saying no to the feminine mystique and organizing to confront sex discrimination was only the first stage. We have somehow to transcend the polarities of the first stage, and even the rage of our own "no," to get to the second stage. (40)

The first stage, the women's movement, was fought within, and against, and defined by that old structure of unequal, polarized male and female roles. But to continue reacting against that structure is still to be defined and limited by its terms. What's needed now is to transcend those terms, transform the structure itself. (40)

Again, it is not the pragmatic answers, but the methodological questions of Friedan's (feminist self-)critique which I find compelling, and most eloquently pertinent to a rethinking of the woman question.

For my part, I would like to channel Friedan's appeal—as she does not—to the specific topic of the relationship between psychoanalysis and feminism. I would like to propose an approach that would take into account both what we can learn (far beyond what has been learned) from psychoanalysis about femininity and what we can learn from the feminist critique about psychoanalysis, in a way that would transcend the reified polarization of these two (as yet unfinished) lessons.

II

Freud and the Woman Question

Freud knew, and said, that his speculative theories of femininity were but provisional. For him, psychoanalysis was not so much an answer (the answers were provisional), as the constant and unfinished struggle to articulate—to open up—a question; a question whose revolutionary implications I believe neither women nor psychoanalysis has as yet measured; a question that he was the first to ask, the first not to take for granted: "What does a woman want?"[5]

Let us pause a moment and reflect: let us try to grasp the creatively outrageous, visionary, revolutionary imagination that it must have taken to historically articulate this question as a *serious* question. Let us listen to the question. Let us listen to its unheard confession and to its unheard of challenge.

What does a woman want? Doesn't everybody *know* what a woman wants? Doesn't what a *woman* wants go without saying? In a patriarchal society, what *can* a woman want except—as everybody knows—to be a mother, daughter, wife? What *can* a woman want except to be protected, loved by man? And what can a woman want in Freud's own eyes except—as every feminist well knows—to have and/or to be the phallus, to realize—in one way or another—her *Penisneid?* And yet, Freud asks. Freud asks, and for the first time in the history of ideas, not just the common sense-defying question: "What *is* a woman?" telling us for the first time that we *do not know* what a woman is, that, counter to all conventional expectations, "what constitutes masculinity or femininity is an unknown characteristic which anatomy cannot lay hold of."[6] Freud also puts in question, puts in focus, woman's *want* as the unresolved problem of psychoanalysis and, by implication, as the unresolved problem of patriarchy, telling us, again, that *we do not know* what a woman really wants. Presumably what a woman wants is of utmost importance. Presumably what a woman really wants is something altogether different than what patriarchy prescribes for her, assumes to be her "natural" desire: otherwise, there is no room for such a question.

"The great question," says Freud to Marie Bonaparte, "the great question that has never been answered and which I have not been able to answer, despite my thirty years of research into the feminine soul, is 'What does a woman want?'"

I propose now to explore, in Freud's text, not so much the answers (tentative and speculative) but the very crisis, the very critical explosion of the question. I propose to search the way Freud *lived* the question, and lived out its crisis, by turning, now, not to any speculative essay on femininity or female sexuality, not to any Freudian theoretical pronouncement, but to a *dream:* Freud's dream of Irma, reported and interpreted in chapter 2 of *The Interpretation of Dreams.* It was the very first dream Freud submitted to detailed interpretation, and he historically derived the theory of dreams from it.[7] I turn to this dream, which, in yielding thus a key to dreams, in triggering Freud's greatest insight into dream interpretation, can be said to be the very dream from which psychoanalysis proceeds, because it also is a dream about femininity, and about Freud's relationship—professional and personal—to femininity. It is thus the singular confession of a singular male dream of singular theoretical and pragmatic consequences. Perhaps it is significant that the relationship of Freud to women is precisely questioned in, and is the focus of, the very crisis dream from which psychoanalysis proceeds.

In turning to this dream, however, I do not mean simply to seize upon a "royal road" to Freud's unconscious so as to attempt reductively—as has become quite fashionable—to "outsmart" Freud in his own psychoanalysis, to psychoanalyze the dream and use it against Freud in a demystifying manner,[8] but rather, and quite differently, I mean to follow up on Freud's advice given in another context: "This," wrote Freud at the end of his theoretical essay on "Femininity," "is all I have to say to you about femininity. It is certainly incomplete and fragmentary and does not always sound friendly. . . . *If you want to know more about femininity, enquire from your own experiences of life, or turn to the poets, or wait until science can give you deeper and more coherent information*" (22:135).

I do indeed want to know more, and I propose to learn more—from Freud himself. In turning here to Freud not as theoretician but as dreamer, and as interpreter of his own dream, it seems to me I am precisely taking Freud's advice to interrogate at once experience,[9] poetry, and science: I am precisely turning to a poet (writer), to a scientist (dream interpreter), and to the life experience of a man who lives out (dreams, and dreams of solving) the questions and contradictions of sexual difference in the concrete dailiness of his material—and creative—life.

The Story of the Dream

Let us now refresh our memory of the dream itself and of its circumstances. The evening before the dream was dreamed (July 23, 1895), Freud met a colleague and friend, Otto, who had just returned from a summer resort where he had met a young woman called Irma, who was Freud's patient. Irma's treatment had been partially successful: she was cured of hysterical anxiety but not of certain somatic symptoms. Before going on vacation Freud had offered Irma an interpretation—a "solution"—of the riddle of her symptoms, but Irma had been unwilling or unable to accept it; and the symptoms persisted. To Freud's question about how Otto had found the patient in that summer resort, Otto replied: "Better, but not quite well," words in which Freud detected a reproach. So as to justify himself, Freud that evening wrote out an explanation of his views on Irma's illness, in the form of a case history addressed to Dr. M., the leading figure in the medical circle at the time and a common friend of Otto and Freud. These circumstances were followed by the dream:

> A large hall—numerous guests, whom we were receiving.—Among them was Irma. I at once took her on one side, as though to answer her letter and to reproach her for not having accepted my "solution" yet. I said to her: "If you still get pains, it's really only your fault." She replied: "If you only knew what pains I've got now in my throat and stomach and abdomen—it's choking me"—I was alarmed and looked at her. She looked pale and puffy. I thought to myself that after all I must be missing some organic trouble. I took her to the window and looked down her throat, and she showed signs of recalcitrance, like women with artificial dentures. I thought to myself that there was really no need for her to do that.—She then opened her mouth properly and on one side I found a big white patch; at another place I saw extensive whitish grey scabs upon some remarkably curly structures which were evidently modelled on the turbinal bones of the nose.—I at once called in Dr. M., and he repeated the examination and confirmed it. . . . Dr. M. looked quite different than usual; he was very pale, he walked with a limp and his chin was clean shaven. . . . My

friend Otto was now standing beside her as well, and my friend
Leopold was percussing her through her bodice and saying: "She
has a dull area low down on the left." He also indicated that a
portion of the skin on the left shoulder was infiltrated. (I noticed
this, just as he did, in spite of her dress.) . . . M. said: "There's no
doubt it's an infection, but no matter; dysentery will supervene
and the toxin will be eliminated." . . . We were directly aware,
too, of the origin of the infection. Not long before, when she was
feeling unwell, my friend Otto had given her an injection of a
preparation of propyl, propyls . . . propionic acid . . . trimethylamin (and I saw before me the formula for this printed in
heavy type). . . . Injections of that sort ought not to be made so
thoughtlessly. . . . And probably the syringe had not been clean
(4:107)

The pragmatic interpretation of the dream—through the chain
of associations it evokes in Freud—is oriented toward the pathbreaking theoretical conclusion posited, at the end, as the basic
thesis of Freud's book: that dreams have a meaning, and that their
meaning is the fulfillment of a wish. "I became," writes Freud,

aware of an intention which was carried into effect by the dream
and which must have been my motive for dreaming it. The dream
fulfilled certain wishes which were started in me by the events of
the previous evening (the news given me by Otto and my writing
out of the case history). The conclusion of the dream, that is to
say, was that I was not responsible for the persistence of Irma's
pains, but that Otto was. Otto had in fact annoyed me by his
remarks about Irma's incomplete cure, and the dream gave me my
revenge by throwing the reproach back onto him. The dream
acquitted me of the responsibility for Irma's condition by showing
that it was due to other factors—it produced a whole series of
reasons. The dream represented a particular state of affairs as I
should have wished it to be. *Thus its content was the fulfillment of a
wish and its motive was a wish.* (4:119)

Let us now return to our central question here, concerning the
relationships of Freud to women and, through them, his relation
to the question of femininity. Apparently, Irma is the only female
figure in the dream. But as the chain of associations reveals, Irma

is in fact the condensation of three different women representing, with respect to Freud, three different sorts of feminine relations. I will now try to organize the associative material related to these three female figures in a somewhat more coherent and more structured manner than the one immediately apparent in Freud's own haphazard, chronological exposition. As I relay this more consistent narrative of the dream's associations, many interpretive connections that Freud deliberately chooses to leave in the dark and not to comment on, not to make explicit, will become apparent. This exposition of the dream material will thus anticipate already, in a sketchy manner, the outline for a possible interpretation. Here, then, is the structured female trio condensed in Irma and the related interpretive information that comes up in Freud's associations.

The First Female Figure: The Young, Recalcitrant Woman Patient—Irma Herself

Irma, a young widow, is characterized in the dream by her complaint (her pains), and her resistance, her unwillingness to accept Freud's solution. Through her "recalcitrance" she is doubled, however, by the image of another young woman patient, a governess who "seemed a picture of youthful beauty, but when it came to opening her mouth she had taken measures to conceal her plates" (4:109). It is thus the incongruous feature of the false teeth and the examination of Irma's oral cavity which brings to Freud's mind the past examination of the governess, as well as "recollections of other medical examinations and of little secrets revealed in the course of them" (4:109).

The feature of the masculine medical examination of female cavities, unveiling and penetrating female secrets, can be related to the later part of the dream, in which Irma is examined and percussed by a group of male doctors, and her symptoms—this time an infection, an "infiltration" in the shoulder—are perceived and diagnosed through, "in spite of her dress." Follow the associations:

In spite of her dress. . . . . We naturally used to examine the children in the hospital undressed: and this would be a contrast to the manner in which adult female patients have to be examined. I remembered that it was said of a celebrated clinician that he never made a physical examination of his patients except through their clothes. Further than this I could not see. Frankly, I had no desire to penetrate more deeply at this point. (4:113)

Later still, when it is discovered that Irma's infection or "infiltration" was caused by an injection given her by Otto with a dirty syringe, Freud's associations evoke two contradictory experiences in his medical treatment of women patients: on the one hand, his tragic, guilty experience with a woman patient named Mathilde (like his eldest daughter), whom Freud had inadvertently killed by prescribing a remedy that was at the time regarded as harmless; and on the other hand, his innocent, felicitous experience with an old lady to whom for two years Freud had given injections with no ill effect. Having learned by chance, the day before the dream, that the old lady was now suffering from phlebitis, Freud at once assumes that "it must be an infiltration caused by a dirty syringe," and is proud that he himself was never guilty of such malpractice: "I was proud of the fact that in two years I had not caused a single infiltration; I took constant pains to be sure that the syringe was clean" (4:118).

The Second Female Figure behind Irma: The Ideal, Phantasmic Woman Patient—Irma's Friend

"The way in which Irma stood by the window," writes Freud, "reminded me of another experience":

Irma had an intimate woman friend of whom I had a very high opinion. When I visited this lady one evening I had found her by a window in the situation reproduced in the dream, and her physician, the same Dr. M., had pronounced that she had a diphteric membrane. . . . It now occurred to me that for the last few months I had had every reason to suppose that this other lady was also a hysteric. Indeed, Irma herself had betrayed the fact to me. What did I know of her condition? One thing precisely: that, like my

Irma of the dream, she suffered from hysterical choking. So in the dream I had replaced my patient by her friend. I now recollected that I had often played with the idea that she too might ask me to relieve her of her symptoms. I myself, however, had thought this unlikely, since she was of a very reserved nature. She was *recalcitrant*, as was shown in the dream. Another reason was that *there was no need for her to do it:* she had so far shown herself strong enough to master her condition without outside help. . . . What could the reason have been for my having exchanged her in the dream for her friend? Perhaps it was that I should have *liked* to exchange her: either I felt more sympathetic towards her friend or had a higher opinion of her intelligence. For Irma seemed to me foolish because she had not accepted my solution. Her friend would have been wiser, that is to say she would have yielded sooner. She would have then *opened her mouth properly*, and have told me more than Irma. (4:110)

Like Irma, Irma's friend is "also a young widow" (4:117).

The Third Female Figure behind Irma: Freud's Wife

There still remained a few features that I could not attach either to Irma or to her friend: *pale; puffy; false teeth.* . . . I then thought of someone else to whom these features might be alluding. She again was not one of my patients, nor should I have liked to have her as a patient, since I had noticed that she was bashful in my presence and I could not think she would make an amenable patient. She was usually pale, and once, while she had been in specially good health, she had looked puffy. Thus I had been comparing my patient Irma to two other people who would also have been recalcitrant to treatment. (4:110)

The text does not spell out the identity of this "someone else," this third female figure who "again was not one of my patients"; but a footnote called forth by the nostalgic mention "once, while she had been in specially good health, she had looked puffy" reads: "The person in question was, *of course*, my own wife" [emphasis mine]. In the footnote, too, another unexplained complaint of Irma finds explanation (it is, in fact, the wife's complaint), although the explanation itself is not explicated:

The still unexplained complaint about *pains in the abdomen* could also be traced back to this third figure. The person in question was, of course, my own wife; the pains in the abdomen reminded me of one of the occasions on which I had noticed her bashfulness. I was forced to admit to myself that I was not treating either Irma or my wife very kindly in this dream; but it should be observed by way of excuse that I was measuring them both by the standard of the good and amenable patient. (4:110)

What Freud omits to tell us, here, is the crucial fact that his wife is, at the time of the dream, *pregnant*,[10] a predicament that can perhaps better explain her "complaint" of "pains in the abdomen and in the stomach."

Although his wife's current pregnancy is never mentioned by Freud, her pregnant condition reappears in a different context of the dream's associations, in connection with the dirty syringe. Immediately after having congratulated himself on the clean syringe with which he gave injections to the old lady, who now was suffering from phlebitis due, perhaps, to the dirty syringe of another doctor, Freud notes: "The phlebitis brought me back once more to my wife, who had suffered from thrombosis during one of her pregnancies" (4:118). The wife is also present in the beginning of the dream, implicit in the words "we were receiving." The dream was dreamed, as the associations tell us, "a few days before my wife's birthday" (4:108), anticipating the birthday party. The birthday celebrated in the background is perhaps implicitly related, in its turn, to the experience of *giving birth*, that is, to the wife's unmentioned pregnancy and to the birth the wife will soon give to Freud's child.

"Ladies and Gentlemen": Freud's Structure of Address

What, then, is the dream telling us about Freud and women? It is easy—all too easy and too tempting—to submit the dream to the traditional hostile and antagonistic feminist approach to Freud, that is, to submit to a *critical* interpretation—to submit to our new feminine awareness and self-awareness—Freud's positions and propositions with respect to the women of the dream. I will first outline this kind of reading below and then attempt to show the limitations of such a traditional feminist approach. I outline, in other words, the critical *first stage* of a feminist interpretation, only with a view toward the further possibilities of a *second-stage* (or a third-stage) approach.

"Ladies and Gentlemen," wrote Freud, at the well-known opening of his theoretical lecture on "Femininity,"

> Today's lecture . . . deals with a subject which has a claim on your interest second almost to no other. Throughout history people have knocked their heads against the riddle of the nature of femininity. . . .
>
> Nor will *you* have escaped worrying over this problem, those of you who are men; as for the women among you this will not apply—they *are* themselves this riddle. (22:113)[11]

In the previous chapters, I have discussed the problematic contradiction inherent in this male structure of address, the discrepancy between Freud's statement opening up the question *of* the woman and his utterance closing it *for* women, excluding women from the question. Freud's address is obviously a rhetorical tease, but Freud is blind to the fact that his tease—his enunciation— unwittingly *represses* what his statement strives to *liberate*, to open up against so many prejudiced and conventional expectations. Freud's rhetorical address seems to imply that the question of femininity, while *involving* women ("they *are* themselves this riddle"), in effect *addresses* only men. The question of femininity becomes thus, in effect, a question of *complicity* among men: a question of the complicity of men about the fact that the question of the Woman is *their* exclusive question.

It is interesting to note that, in its very different setting, the Irma dream inscribes, dramatically, the very same *male* structure of address which "Femininity" inscribes theoretically and pedagogically.

It is to Dr. M.—"the leading figure in our circle"—that Freud, in waking life, addresses Irma's case report; and in the dream, when Irma's suffering defies and threatens Freud's "solution," it is to male authority that Freud appeals: "I at once called in Dr. M., and he repeated the examination and confirmed it." The riddle of the woman—Irma's body, or Irma's riddle—is thus submitted to an exclusively male examination: "My friend Otto was now standing beside her . . . and my friend Leopold was percussing her through her bodice. . . . M. said: 'There's no doubt it's an infection. . . .' We were directly aware, too, of the origin of the infection." Here again the question of femininity becomes a question of male knowledge, a knowledge whose authority is ratified by male complicity. Irma does not speak, whereas the male group speaks *about* her, but not *to* her. The riddle, it would seem, "does not apply" to Irma *because* "she is herself the riddle."

The Question of Male Insight

Commenting on "the habitual masculine bias of Freud's own terms and diction,"[12] Kate Millet notes very judiciously, in reference to the whole corpus of Freud's writing:

> One is struck by how thoroughly the subjectivity in which all these events are cast tends to be Freud's own, or that of a strong masculine bias, even of a rather gross male supremacist bias. (247)

> [Freud] himself seemed incapable of *imagining objectivity* as a non-masculine related quality. (273)

This is absolutely true and probably has not been, and is not, sufficiently acknowledged by mainstream psychoanalysis to date. There is a basic given of psychoanalytic theory, that psychoanalytic theory has as yet to learn how to take into account: Freud's is a *male genius*. Freud is a male genius.

This may sound like a simple statement. Yet I contend that we do not yet know what this statement really means. It certainly *does not mean* that Freud's stupendous insight is disqualified as far as women are concerned, or that his genius is irrelevant to women (or to feminism); it *does mean* (but in what way?) that his insight is inhabited by certain systematic oversights, and that the light it sheds also casts shadows.

The question, then, the real challenge that will keep confronting feminists who wish to be informed—or inspired—by psychoanalysis, is how to work *with* Freud's male genius, and not simply *against* it, as the feminist tradition felt compelled to do in its beginnings: whereas the first-stage feminism simply blocked, *foreclosed* male insights because of the (necessarily prejudicial) bias of their male enunciation, what we have not finished learning and what, in my view, we will never finish learning is, on the contrary, how to *relate*—in ever new ways—to a male genius: how to work *within* male insights so as to displace their oversights not from without, but from within, in such a way as to learn from their inspiration, and thus derive fresh (female) insights from their past conceptions.

The Anxiety of Paternity

Let us, then, return to the dream and to its "first-stage"[13] feminist interpretation. We have seen that in the dream Irma's riddle is submitted to a male examination. But Freud has told us, in that crucial and peculiar footnote, that his wife is also present behind Irma. What is then the role, and the significance, of Freud's wife in and for the dream? Monique Schneider, one of the subtlest French interpreters of Freud among those who submit Freud to a feminist critique, suggests that if the "possible allusion to the unborn child as the fruit of the unclean syringe" links the whole dream to the idea of maternity, then the expression "the toxin will be eliminated" is "disquieting," because the "purgative elimination" can be symbolically equated with "infanticide."[14] "Freud," writes Schneider, "had doubtless the feeling of having abandoned, inside the body of his wife, a part of his own substance, of his own 'solution'" (143). The dream is thus "the expression of a refused paternity, a paternity cleaned away" (133). "How," asks Monique Schneider, "could paternity be transformed into an infanticidal operation?" And she answers: "In the dream, the necessity of a maternal mediation—the patient has to 'accept the solution'—may account for the vindictive movement which would like to liquefy the belly interposing itself, in paternity, between the action proper of the father and the product of his action. . . . The woman constitutes a screen, an obstacle in the realization of a creative omnipotence; the wife as well as the patient are accused of not offering themselves as purely receptive matrixes" (134). Thus, the dream's purgative intention stands, in Schneider's interpretation, for a "matricidal and infanticidal fury" (133).

Perhaps Schneider's interpretation can explain the fact that Freud took such care to repress rhetorically, never to mention, his wife's pregnancy. "I have now completed the interpretation of the dream," writes Freud, and in a footnote (written ten years later) adds: "Though it will be understood that I have not reported everything that occurred to me during the process of interpretation" (4:118). "I will not pretend," Freud recapitulates toward the chapter's end,

> that I have completely uncovered the meaning of the dream or that its interpretation is without a gap. I could spend much more time over it, derive further information from it and discuss fresh problems raised by it. I myself know the points from which further trains of thought could be followed. But considerations which arise in the case of every dream of my own restrain me from pursuing my interpretive work. If anyone should feel tempted to express a hasty condemnation of my reticence, I would advise him to make the experiment of being franker than I am. (4:121)

If Schneider perhaps uncovers what Freud hides, it is, however, in the tradition of the feminist approach, so as to reverse, symmetrically, the image of Freud the hero into that of Freud the villain. The interpretation is not carried out so as to explore an insight (for instance, the significance of infanticidal fantasies in mental life, or the complexity and ambiguity of human creativity) but rather so as to pronounce a moral condemnation, to set Freud on trial and to set up a Manischaeistic world picture in which human beings are divided into two clearly defined, symmetrically and diametrically opposed camps: men/women; aggressors/victims; villains/heroines; "the bad"/"the good". Indeed, in spite of her remarkable finesse and penetrating analytic mind, Monique Schneider cannot but fall into this Manichaeistic trap. To borrow, once again, Betty Friedan's pertinent expressions, this is doubtless not "the feminine mystique"; but is it not a *feminist mystique?*

Competing Pregnancies

In the same line of interpreting the pregnancy—and the presence of Freud's wife—as the dream's center, Erik Erikson proposes a different reading,[15] more sympathetic to the dreamer's male point of view. "Freud," writes Erikson, "had the Irma dream when he was about to enter the fifth decade of his life, to which we would ascribe the generativity crisis" (IYC 197), the crisis of middle age: "an age when he seemed to notice with alarm the first signs of aging, and in fact, of disease; burdened with the responsibility for a fast-growing family" (IYC 199):

> [It was] a time when his wife was again expecting and when he himself stood before a major emancipation as well as the "germination" of a major idea. (DS 41)

> At the time of this dream, then, he knew that he would have to bear a great discovery—and "bear" here has a "pregnant" double meaning. (IYC 199)

> The Irma dream is concerned with a middle-aged man's cares, with the question of how much of what he has started he can also take care of, and whether or not he is not at times too careless to be able to sustain his ambitions. (IYC 197)

Erikson's interpretation is indeed ingenious: the Irma dream is dealing with the *competing pregnancies* of Freud—pregnant with psychoanalysis—and of his wife—pregnant with their child.

However, Erikson relates, still more ingeniously and through an absolutely brilliant insight, the paradoxical predicament of Freud's own pregnancy with the presence, in the dream, of Freud's friend and supporter, Fliess, evoked by Freud in association with the formula of trimethylamine.[16] (It should be remembered—in the background—that it is from Fliess that Freud derived the theory of bisexuality.) Here then is Erikson's interpretation:

> The "mouth which opens wide" . . . is not only the oral cavity of a patient and not only a symbol of woman's procreative inside, which arouses horror and envy because it can produce new "formations." It is also the investigator's oral cavity, opened to medical inspection; and it may well represent, at the same time, the dreamer's unconscious, soon to offer insights never faced before to an idealized friend with the hope that (here we must read the whole dream backwards) *wir empfangen:* we receive, we conceive, we celebrate a birthday. That a man may incorporate another man's spirit, that a man may conceive from another man, and that a man may be reborn from another, these ideas are the content of many fantasies and rituals which mark significant moments of male initiation, conversion and inspiration; and every act of creation, at one stage, implies the unconscious fantasy of inspiration by a fertilizing agent of a more or less deified, more or less personified mind or spirit. (DS 48)

But if, as Erikson magnificently analyzes, the Irma dream is transferentially *addressed to* Fliess; if Freud is seeking to conceive psychoanalysis from Fliess—or with Fliess—rather than to concentrate on his child's conception with his wife, then the dream repeats, once more, the exclusion of the woman, the homosexual complicity, the male supremacist structure of address, even with respect to this most female theme of pregnancy, of *conception.*

"Women," as indeed Freud writes in *Civilization and Its Discontents,*

> represent the interests of family and the sexual life; the work of civilization has become more and more men's business; it confronts them with ever more difficult tasks and compels them to carry out instinctual sublimations of which women are little capable. Since a man does not have unlimited quantities of psychical energy at his disposal, he has to accomplish his tasks by making an expedient distribution of his libido. What he employs for cultural aims he to a great extent withdraws from women and sexual life.

His constant association with men, and his dependence on his relation with them, even estrange him from his duties as a husband and father. Thus the woman finds herself forced into the background by the claims of civilization and she adopts a hostile attitude towards it. (21:103–4)

This sexual separation—this mutual discontent of the sexes toward each other within the normative prescriptions of a patriarchal social structure—may be seen as the very issue of the Irma dream.

Paternalistic Medicine

The claims of patriarchal structure are, indeed, dramatized by the dream not just on the personal-familial level, but on the professional-medical level as well. Not only are all the doctors male and all the patients female: the "recalcitrant" female patient is treated by the self-righteous and paternalistic doctor like a stubborn child. The rapport between doctor and patient thus perpetuates the hierarchical male/female, father/child subordinating opposition in a medical frame apparently structured by a master-slave relationship. On this basis, Sarah Kofman, still another French feminist interpreter of Freud, writes, in reference to the Irma dream: "The irreducible women who refuse to open up their mouth"—their oral cavity—"because they do not accept the pernicious 'solution' of their psychoanalyst, will be . . . soon abandoned by him, quickly substituted by this man whose tenderness is reserved only to 'sympathetic,' likable women, those who properly open their mouth, those whom he finds 'wiser,' 'more intelligent' because they better know how to follow his advice, accept his solutions. . . . It is always the ladies' fault. . . . The dream is a veritable defense counsel's speech in favor of Freud's innocence."[17]

"But if Freud experiences such a need to disculpate himself," Kofman argues, "it is because he is, himself, the criminal. Not only because he has not yet cured Irma, but . . . because he has himself (a fault which is displaced in the dream and its interpretation onto his friend Otto) rendered her ill, because he has himself infected her with his symbolico-spermatic solution of . . . trimethylamine injected with a dirty syringe. . . If Irma and all the irreducible women refuse to open their mouth and genitals, it is because Freud has already . . . closed their mouth, rendered them frigid, by injecting them with an erudite and malignant male solution. What else would they still have to say or to reveal, if not . . . that they were contaminated by him who, under the pretext of curing them, constrains them to collaborate, because he needs their complicity in order to believe, himself, in the value of his 'solution'" (56–57).

"The psychoanalytic solution," Kofman concludes, "restores speech to the woman only in order then better to despoil her of it, better to subjugate this speech to the discourse of the master" (57).

Reading and Anger

Again, we are confronted, in this single-minded feminist interpretation, on the one hand, with an angry female reading and, on the other hand, with a Freud who has become, once more, a villain and a culprit.

Such rage, unfortunately, is self-blinding. As a woman, I cannot but understand the anger. But as a reader, I cannot but deplore the way in which I see the anger miss its mark, miss its own critical objectives in sliding toward a caricature—both of Freud and of itself.

The trouble with such mystifying demystifications is that they do to Freud precisely what they claim Freud does to women: they close the mouth of Freud's text: they judge, but they do not listen. Having decided in advance upon the "closure" of Freud's text, they paradoxically realize this closure through their own impermeability to the male insight of the text. "Battles won or lost," writes Betty Friedan, "are being fought in terms that are somehow inadequate, irrelevant. . . . And yet the larger revolution,

evolution, liberation . . . has hardly begun. How do we move on? What are the terms of the second stage?" (*Second Stage*, 27).

To restate the question in terms of my own concerns here: how can we account *at the same time* for the text's *male blindness* and for the text's *male insight* (its very textual otherness to its blindness)? How can we engage in a dialogue at once with the blindness *and* with the insight of Freud's text?

A Self-Ironic Statement

What, indeed, does the traditional feminist critique fail to see, above all, in the Irma dream? It fails to see the fact (which, like "the Purloined Letter," is "a little too self-evident" to be perceived)[18] that Freud has made it all too easy for us women to attack him in this way because *he said it all himself*, explicitly. The text *invites* this feminist critique, invites it not through its blind spots but, on the contrary, through its most conscious, and self-conscious, statements. The "first-stage" feminist critique, in other words, is first and foremost Freud's male *self-critique*.

Indeed, the first-stage feminist critique precisely fails to read, in Freud, that very aspect of his text which should, in my opinion, be regarded as his greatest—his most inspiring and thought-provoking—contribution to a feminist reflection: the crucially self-critical, self-questioning, and self-ironical potential, and activity, of his text. The Irma dream is, on the whole, a *self-ironic* statement: Freud's subtle, but ever present irony toward himself constantly calls into question his own assumptions, his own certainties, his own male consciousness—and consciousness as such.

> *I reproached Irma for not having accepted my solution; I said: "If you still get pains, it's your own fault."* . . . It was my view at the time (though *I have since recognized it was a wrong one*) that my task was fulfilled when I had informed a patient of the hidden meaning of his symptoms: I considered that I was not responsible for whether he accepted the solution or not—though this was what success depended on. *I owe it to this mistake*, which I have now *fortunately corrected, that my life was made easier* at a time when, in spite of all

my inevitable ignorance, I was expected to produce therapeutic successes. (4:108; emphasis mine)

Kofman's reading does not in effect analyze the dream but paraphrases it—incompletely, echoing but one of its many voices. Paradoxically enough, in blaming Freud for his repressive and reductive male *appropriation* of female speech, what Kofman is precisely doing is (selectively, reductively) *appropriating* Freud's own words.

But the symmetry, here as elsewhere, is misleading. For in seemingly reversing Freud's appropriative gesture, Kofman fails to see that the Irma dream is not simply a description of Freud's attempt at mastery; it is a description, a dramatization, of the necessary failure of such an attempt: the Irma dream is, on the contrary, a recognition of the *impasse* (medical and sexual) inherent in the very impulse to appropriate, to forcefully reduce the otherness of the other.

And this is why the Irma dream is a key dream that, in the search that was to be psychoanalysis, yields the fruit of the discovery not just of wish fulfillment and of the theory of dreams, but of the question of *resistance* as a psychoanalytic question (as yet unexplored, unformulated, but obscurely grasped, intuited). The dream's discovery, in other words, is that of the necessity, precisely, of *transforming*, in psychoanalysis, the master-slave relationship. The dream articulates the necessity of breaking away from the prescriptions of the medical patriarchal frame and the conventional professional relationship that structure it.

An Oneiric Lesson of Self-Difference

In waking life, Freud indeed desired to *reduce resistance* and specifically, resistance to his male or medical or intellectual "solutions". But the dream, precisely, dramatizes, through the insistent "recalcitrance" of women both as lovers and as patients, something like a *resistance of resistance:* it is the dream itself that seems to be resisting Freud's daytime, waking attitudes; it is not simply women but the dream, Freud's dream, which seems to be resisting Freud's solutions, as well as Freud's resistance to resistance. The solutions *of* the dream are, in other words, altogether different from the solutions *in* the dream. The dream is looking for a solution altogether different from the imposition of solutions which it dramatizes.

If the dream comes up, precisely, with the notion of *wish fulfillment* as the meaning (the *solution*) of the dream—of any dream—it is perhaps because Freud realizes that his past solutions were but wish fulfillments, dream solutions. "The unconscious," says Lacan, "is precisely the hypothesis that one does not dream only when one sleeps"(5). But, says Freud, if we do indeed have an unconscious, if we do not dream only when we are asleep, is it possible that the dream itself could have a *waking function?* Is it possible that sleep itself could *wake us up* from our daily dream of wakefulness? Is it possible, in other words, that a dream—in sleep—would sound the alarm of daytime false solutions?

This, it seems to me, is what is at stake in the Irma dream, dealing as it does with the inadequacy of waking (sexual and medical) male solutions. The dream—and this is why it is a dream of genius: a dream that speaks *beyond* Freud's ego, beyond Freud's present knowledge, beyond Freud's narcissistic male self-consciousness and consciousness—the dream is *critical* of Freud's life attitudes: but critical in a creative way: a way that opens up a "royal road" to a pathbreaking innovation, a way whose very *dead end*—the deadlock dramatized by the dream—will bring about a revolutionary *breakthrough*. And this is why the Irma dream—the dream, precisely, of the awkwardness of Freud's patriarchal encounter with feminine resistance, the very dream of the inadequacy of Freud's male solutions to the feminine complaint—will end up giving birth to the *displaced* solution of a revolutionary kind of listening: of listening—differently and differentially—at once to others and to oneself; of listening—differently and differentially—to one's own dream. And Freud, indeed, had listened to the crisis, to the question of the dream. And this is why the Irma dream—this critical, historical inscription of male blindness and male genius—will end up giving birth to the displaced solution of a revolutionary theory of sexual difference, that is, of sexuality not just as difference but as *self-difference*. And this is why the Irma dream—Freud's dream of femininity, of sexuality, of difference—has turned out to be, in all the senses of the word, the very *dream* from which, in an undreamed of manner, psychoanalysis was born.

III

Jokes and Their Relation to the Unconscious

In an unprecedented flash of insight, Freud discovers that the purpose of the dream lies in the direction of wish fulfillment. What, however, is the status of that wish fulfillment? "The dream," writes Freud, "acquitted me of the responsibility for Irma's condition by showing that it was due to other factors—it produced a whole series of reasons":

> I noticed, it is true, that these explanations of Irma's pains (which agreed in exculpating me) were not entirely consistent with one another and indeed that they were mutually exclusive. The whole plea—for the dream was nothing else—reminded one vividly of the defence put forward by the man who was charged by one of his neighbours with having given him back a borrowed kettle in a damaged condition. The defendant asserted first, that he had given it back undamaged; secondly, that the kettle had a hole in it when he borrowed it; and thirdly, that he had never borrowed a kettle from his neighbour at all. So much the better: if only a single one of these three lines of defence were to be accepted as valid, the man would have to be acquitted. (4:119)

The dreamlike wish fulfillment thus partakes of the unconscious logic of a joke. And indeed, in *Jokes and Their Relation to the Unconscious*, Freud returns twice to this "piece of sophistry"—this joke of the borrowed kettle—and discusses it again in relation to the logic of the Irma dream, which, like this joke, does not admit the "either-or" alternative.

The story of the borrowed kettle which had a hole in it when it was given back is an excellent example of the purely comic effect giving free play to the unconscious mode of thought. It will be recalled that the borrower, when he was questioned, replied firstly that he had not borrowed a kettle at all, secondly, that it had had a hole in it already when he had borrowed it, and thirdly, that he had given it back undamaged and without a hole. This mutual canceling out by several thoughts, each of which is in itself valid, is precisely what does not occur in the unconscious. In dreams, in which the modes of thought of the unconscious are actually manifest, there is accordingly no such thing as an "either-or," only a simultaneous juxtaposition.

In the example of a dream which, in spite of its complication, I chose in my *Interpretation of Dreams* as a specimen of the work of interpretation, I tried to rid myself of the reproach of having failed to relieve a patient of her pains by psychical treatment. My reasons were: (1) that she herself was responsible for her illness because she would not accept my solution, (2) that her pains were of organic origin and were therefore no concern of mine, (3) that her pains were connected with her widowhood, for which I was evidently not responsible and (4) that her pains were due to an injection from a contaminated syringe, which had been given her by someone else. All these reasons stood side by side, as though they were not mutually exclusive. I was obliged to replace the "and" of the dream by an "either-or" in order to escape a charge of nonsense. (8:205)

In confronting Freud, however, with the "either-or" alternatives and symmetrical dichotomies of a Manichaeistic worldview, and in taking literally the oneiric statement of Freud's wish fulfillment as the homogeneously one-sided, self-identical statement of the dream, the first-stage feminist critique precisely misses the wish fulfillment's—and the text's—status as a joke. "The faulty reasoning," writes Freud, "which [the joke] uses for its technique as one of the modes of thought of the unconscious, *strikes criticism . . . as being comic. . . . * A joke which makes use of faulty reasoning like this for its technique, and therefore appears nonsensical, can thus produce a comic effect at the same time. *If we fail to detect the joke*, we are once again left only with the comic or funny story" (8:204–5, emphasis mine). If the first-stage feminist interpreters are "left," indeed, only with the *senselessness* of Freud's own narrative—"only with the comic or funny story" of Freud's oneiric wish fulfillment—it is because they fail, precisely, to detect the wish fulfillment's status as a joke.

What, however, is the purpose of the joke? And why have women so systematically missed the joke? Is there a relationship between the very act of joking and the predicament of sexual difference?

"The purposes of jokes," writes Freud in the work he dedicates to this discursive genre, "can easily be reviewed": "Where a joke is not an aim in itself—that is, when it is not an innocent one—there are only two purposes that it may serve, and these two can themselves be subsumed under a single heading. It is either a *hostile* joke (serving the purpose of aggressiveness, satire, or defence) or an *obscene* joke (serving the purpose of exposure)" (8:96–97). This last category, which Freud defines as "smut," is then discussed, precisely, in relation to, and as a mode of, the experience of sexual difference.

> We know what is meant by "smut": the intentional bringing into prominence of sexual facts and relations by speech. . . . In spite of this definition, [however,] a lecture on the anatomy of the sexual organs need not have a single point of contact with smut. It is a further relevant fact that smut is directed to a particular person, by whom one is sexually excited and who, on hearing it, is expected to become aware of the speaker's excitement and as a result to become sexually excited in turn. . . . Smut is thus originally directed towards women and may be equated with attempts at seduction. If a man in the company of men enjoys telling or listening to smut, the original situation, which owing to social inhibitions cannot be realized, is at the same time imagined. A person who laughs at smut that he hears is laughing as though he were the spectator of an act of sexual aggression. (8:97)

In much the same way as the Irma dream dramatizes its investigation of sexual difference through the exposure of a female cavity, smut consists in an *exposure of the sexually different person:*

Smut is like an exposure of the sexually different person to whom it is directed. By the utterance of the obscene words it compels the person who is assailed to imagine the part of the body or the procedure in question and shows her that the assailant is himself imagining it. *It cannot be doubted that the desire to see what is sexual exposed is the original motive of smut.* (8:98)

A wooing speech . . . is not yet smut, but it passes over into it. If the woman's readiness emerges quickly the obscene speech has a short life; it yields at once to a sexual action. It is otherwise if quick readiness on the woman's part is not to be counted on, and if in place of it defensive reactions appear. In that case the sexually exciting speech becomes an aim in itself in the shape of smut. (8:99)

In much the same way as the Irma dream proceeds from the feminine resistance to exposure, "the woman's inflexibility is therefore the first condition for the development of smut":

The ideal case of a resistance of this kind on the woman's part occurs if another man is present at the same time—a third person—, for in that case an immediate surrender by the woman is as good as out of the question. This third person soon acquires the greatest importance in the development of smut; to begin with, however, the presence of the woman is not to be overlooked. . . . [But] gradually, in place of the woman, the onlooker, now the listener, becomes the person to whom the smut is addressed, and owing to this transformation it is already near to assuming the character of a joke. (8:99)

In much the same way as the Irma dream—although investigating Irma's body—is addressed to Fliess or to Dr. M., the sexual joke, although originally seeking an exposure of the female body, is in turn motivated in an exclusively *male structure of address:* "to those of you who are women this will not apply—you *are* yourselves the problem." Like the act of theorizing, the act of joking is rhetorically addressed to *male accomplices.*

Generally speaking, a tendentious joke calls for three people: in addition to the one who makes the joke, there must be a second who is taken as the object of the hostile or sexual aggressiveness, and a third in whom the joke's aim of producing pleasure is fulfilled. . . . When the first person finds his libidinal impulse inhibited by the woman, he develops a hostile trend against the second person and calls on the originally interfering third person as an ally. Through the first person's smutty speech the woman is exposed before the third who, as listener, has now been bribed by the effortless satisfaction of his own libido. (8:100)

No wonder, then, that feminists have missed the joke whose logic structures the Irma dream: women do not occupy the place from which the joke is funny. If the joke is an exchange of laughter or of pleasure between two men at the expense of women, women are completely justified to put themselves in a position to *miss the joke.*

It is true that Freud's joke of the borrowed kettle is not exactly smut, nor is it literally—overtly or explicitly—a sexual joke. And yet, as a paradigm for the unconscious logic (or illogic) of the rhetoric of wish fulfillment, the story of the borrowed kettle, insofar as it epitomizes the very structure of the *specimen dream,* turns into something like a *specimen joke,* unwittingly bringing into the interpretive discourse the whole spectrum of aggressive, sexual, and seductive connotations of the rhetoric of jokes.

It is no coincidence, indeed, that the specimen dream, dealing as it does with the predicament of sexual difference, finds itself resolved—and unresolved—by joking. It is no coincidence that joking happens at this juncture of the labor of interpretation of sexuality and difference, and that the joke comes up in Freud's theorization, perhaps less as a comment than as one more dream association.

Unwittingly, the story of the borrowed kettle dramatizes, in its turn, the predicament of sexual difference which the dream, precisely, questions and explores. The kettle, in its phallic and urethral connotations, could be viewed as recapitulating the oneiric image of the syringe and the question of the injection. The hole could, on the other hand, evoke the vision of the female cavity and the oneiric question of the damage ("infiltration" or infection). The question of the joke, in much the same way as the question of the dream, is how to account for the *difference?* How to account for the hole, the loss of bodily integrity, for the (original or inflicted) damage? What is *funny* in the joke, however, is that it refuses to resolve the question of the difference in terms of the logic of identity. The joke thus undercuts the owner's logic, the claim of wholeness: it is impossible to account for the hole in terms of a whole, since the loss of wholeness affects the very meaning of the joke: the joke subverts the self-identity (the wholeness) of its own meaning.

So does, in fact, Freud's dream: "I will not pretend," writes Freud, "that I have completely uncovered the meaning of this dream or that its interpretation is *without a gap*" (4:121). The very meaning of the dream—the stated wish fulfillment—itself is but a kind of borrowed kettle that can somehow never be returned to wholeness.

> The whole plea—for the dream was nothing else—reminded one vividly of the defence put forward by the man who was charged by one of his neighbours with having given him back a borrowed kettle in a damaged condition." (4:119)

The wish fulfillment is a joke. And yet the joke—Freud's joke (in much the same way as Henry James' joke[19])—is in reality a *worry.* The wish fulfillment in effect is nothing other than a *denial* of the (sexual) anxiety of difference and self-difference, which the story of the borrowed kettle all at once materializes and disavows. Indeed, the joking "piece of sophistry" is first and foremost a *defense* against the conflict (crisis, contradiction, and self-contradiction) which provokes, and is embodied by, the dream. "I am aware that these explanations of Irma's illness, which unite in acquitting me, *do not agree with one another;* that they even exclude one another. . . . A *complicated defence,* but so much the better" (4:119–20).[20] The wish fulfillment—"a complicated defence"—is paradoxically enough a denial of the complication, a dream denial of the crisis of the dream, which is not just, in line with Erikson's interpretation, an autobiographical (male generative) crisis but also and perhaps primarily and fundamentally, a *textual crisis.* The "explanations" that pertain to the "defence" (the wish fulfillment) "do not agree with one another" because, below the wish fulfillment and beyond it, Freud's text (Freud's dream) is *far from being in agreement with itself.* In realizing Freud's historic *self-analysis*, the dream itself is not a simple statement of a wish fulfillment but an ongoing, unended, and perhaps unending *analytic dialogue with its own self-difference.* The dream asks: Where is my real wish in all this complication? What do I really want? What do I really want as a man, as a husband, as a doctor, as a future father, and as the future creator of psychoanalysis? The *stated* wish fulfillment fulfills, indeed, the wish less of the doctor (to be disculpated) than of the dream interpreter (to have interpreted the dream). But if the stated wish fulfillment does *fulfill,* it does not *name,* the dream's wish, which is, perhaps, the wish to sort, and to sort out, the very crisis of the wish: the wish to figure out, precisely, the dream's wish.

What Freud, in other words, discovers in the Irma dream is not so much a wish, as the *unconscious* nature of the wish. The founding and pathbreaking psychoanalytic insight that "a dream is the fulfillment of a wish" means, precisely, that a wish, by definition, is *what needs interpretation:* a wish is what cannot be known, directly felt, or *simply stated.*

When the "first-stage" feminist critique takes Freud's *stated* wish fulfillment, that is, his *denial of the crisis* that the dream embodies—his desire to prolong, maintain his sleep[21]—as the simple statement of the drama, of the conflict of the dream, is it seeing in the dream anything but its own (militantly and misguidedly anti-Freudian) wish fulfillment? In saying that this wish fulfillment is "what Freud wants," we simply say that Freud, that night, wanted to *sleep.*[22]

But if Freud that night, and other nights, succumbed to sleep, he was also a unique explorer of human constitutional insomnia. "Wisdom is a sleep deprived of dreams," writes Nietzsche.[23] But Freud was not, in that sense, a good sleeper. Freud's was not, in that sense, a *wise* sleep. And if the Irma dream bears witness to what we may call, indeed, *male sleep*—a narcissistic, wish-fulfilling sleep—it also, at the same time, dramatizes *male insom-*

nia: male restlessness in the face of unsatisfactory male solutions, and the refusal of the sleep—insomniac with dreams—to sleep away the problems.

The challenge, I believe, for feminists today, and the question for a "second-stage" female reinterpretation of Freud's dream, is how to relate differentially to this male dream, by specifically encroaching on, and situating, its male insomnia. The challenge for a "second-stage" feminist and Freudian *dream critique* is, I would suggest, to analyze and to articulate, in male dreams, the female lessons of their male insomnia. By engaging in an analytic dialogue with the dream's self-analytic dialogue, with the dream's own self-debate, with its difference from itself, women should be asking—sympathetically yet critically, critically yet sympathetic- ally—"What does Freud want?" in the same challenging, cre- ative, and imaginative way that Freud has asked: "What does a woman want?"

The Plea and the Complaint

What does Freud want? What does Freud want of women, and with women?

The dream is entirely focused on two features that insistently recur in all the female figures of the dream: resistance, on the one hand (resistance to solutions, recalcitrance to treatment); and on the other hand, suffering, pain, "complaint."[24] It would not be inappropriate to see the entire Irma dream as a dream, specifi- cally, about *female resistance*, and about *female complaint*. Freud is indeed obsessed not just with Irma's nonacceptance of his solu- tion but, even more importantly, with her pain:

> I was not to blame for *Irma's pains*, since she herself was to blame for them. . . . *I* was not concerned with *Irma's pains*, since they were of an organic nature. . . . *Irma's pains* could be satisfactorily explained by her widowhood. . . . *Irma's pains* had been caused by Otto. . . . *Irma's pains* were the result of an injection. . . . I no- ticed, it is true, that all these explanations of *Irma's pains* were not

entirely consistent with one another. . . . The whole *plea*—for the dream was nothing else—reminded one . . . of the defence . . . (4:119)

The oneiric wish fulfillment ("I was not to blame for Irma's pains"), thus partakes not only of the nature of a *joke*, but also, of the nature of a *plea*. A plea, like a joke, is not so much informative, as performative: it is primarily an act—a speech act carried out in *self-defense* and addressing an accuser: "The whole plea—for the dream was nothing else . . ." As this passage clearly indicates, however, the defense is not just a defense against accusation; it is first and foremost a defense against *pain*. What the plea immediately responds to, is obsessed with, is less the veiled reproach of male colleagues than the muter accusation spoken by the very suffering, the very persistence of Irma's pain: Freud's defense against his own vulnerability to the suffering of the other. For Irma, as his patient, has entrusted him with her "complaint."

Now, a complaint is also, like a plea, a speech act that consists in an appeal, in a solicitation of the other: "If you only knew what pains *I've* got. . . . I was alarmed and looked at her." Irma's complaint does not simply *describe* the pain but actively *solicits* the physician, addresses him with her desire for relief. Freud feels *addressed* by Irma's pain. And it is *because* he feels addressed, because he feels addressed and *wounded* by the other's pain, which summons him but only conjures up his impotence as healer—his incapacity to answer effectively the address—that he dreams up this "plea," this drama of "defense," enacting less a play of power seeking to reduce the other than an attempt to ward off pain, to cover up the wound of his own impotence to heal—to reach—the other's wound. The dream thus dramatizes not just a power struggle—the war between the sexes—but the mutual play of the vulnerability of the two sexes: the way in which the state of being wounded by the other sex *addresses* still the other sex: in a *complaint* or in a *plea*.

The drama of the dream consists in a peculiar sexual relation between two central speech acts: "The whole plea—for the dream was nothing else"—is a male plea responding to a crucial female pain, which the defense, in the same movement, strives at once to hear and not to hear, a male plea answering a feminine complaint that the male dreamer knows he misses but that the dream, precisely, strives to comprehend, to be in touch with, to reach out to.

Thus it is that the defensive, wish-fulfilling statement: "I was not concerned with Irma's pains," is an obvious denial, which the dream dramatically belies: not only is Freud metaphorically *suffering through Irma* in the dream: the dream's peculiar logic makes him *literally* suffer through her, when it turns out, during Irma's medical (male) examination, that her painful symptom (in the shoulder) is Freud's own:

> My friend Otto was now standing beside the patient and my friend Leopold was examining her and indicated that there was a dull area low down on the left.
>
> *A portion of the skin on the left shoulder was infiltrated.* I saw at once that this was the rheumatism in my own shoulder, which I invariably notice if I sit up late into the night. Moreover, the wording in the dream was most ambiguous: '*I noticed this, just as he did.*' . . . I noticed it in my own body, that is. (4:112–13)

It is because he hears and feels the woman's suffering within himself, because he finds the feminine complaint inscribed in his own body, that Freud can, for the first time, cure hysteria, relieve—if only partially—Irma's anxiety. "Freud's first interest," writes Lacan, "was in hysteria":

> He spent a lot of time listening, and while he was listening, there resulted something paradoxical, . . . a *reading*. It was while listening to hysterics that he *read* that there was an unconscious. That is, something he could only construct, and in which he himself was implicated; he was implicated in it in the sense that, to his great astonishment, he noticed that he could not avoid participating in what the hysteric was telling him, and that he felt affected by it. Naturally, everything in the resulting rules through which he established the practice of psychoanalysis is designed to counteract this consequence, to conduct things in such a way as to avoid being affected.[25]

Contrary to received opinion, Freud was thus the first to not invalidate but, on the contrary, to listen to, and to devise new ways of listening to, the feminine complaint, even if he could only hear it partially—through his own masculine defenses—and even if what he did hear was then somewhat distorted by his own male vulnerability and by the unavoidable ideological male bias of his own cultural unconscious and of his own male subjectivity.

Between the Patient and the Wife: The Missing Link

How, then, does Freud's wife enter this picture of the confrontation between Freud and Irma, between the plea and the complaint? The significance of the wife's presence is, in my view, crucial not just on her own behalf, but in relation to Irma's feminine complaint. This significance, however, this critical interpretive potential of the possible contamination, of the dreamlike interpenetration of the various feminine complaints, has systematically been overlooked by all previous interpreters and reinterpreters of the dream. On this point, paradoxically enough, female readers meet with male interpreters, from whose interpretations they try to break away but whose oversight they reproduce in failing to articulate—to notice and to bring to consciousness—the crucial *link* between the patient and the wife on which, it seems to me, the question of the dream is founded; an oneiric missing link in which, perhaps, the dream's unconscious wish—as well as its unconscious wish fulfillment—can be located.

It is, indeed, ironically noteworthy that the two feminist interpretations of the dream, perhaps because of their generally polarized and polarizing "either-or" approach, focus their interpretive attention *either* on the patient, Irma (Kofman's reading), *or* on Freud's wife as the future mother of his child (Schneider's interpretation). The same tendency to polarize the women symmetrically, to separate the wife from Irma and to concentrate the analysis on either one or the other of the two, can also be traced back to the two notorious male interpreters of the Irma dream: Erik Erikson and Jacques Lacan.[26]

Interestingly enough, in the male readings, the one-sided emphasis on the wife or on the female patient is explicitly articulated as a denial of the importance of the other female figure. Thus, Erikson, who centers his whole interpretation on Freud's wife and on the importance of her pregnancy, emphasizes the dream's opening—"we were receiving"—as an indication of the (implicitly) visual fact that Freud is naturally "a part of a twosome, his wife and himself." Irma, on the other hand, is for Erikson, with respect to Freud, nothing other than "a complaining and resistive *vis-à-vis*" (emphasis mine). In this perspective, the progression of the dream is described by Erikson as a shrinking away of the central introductory space—the family surroundings—into the pure emptiness of Irma's presence, whom Erikson literally seems not to see: "The dreamer, at first is a *part of a twosome*, his wife and himself, or maybe a family group, vis-à-vis a number of guests. 'We receive,' under festive circumstances in an opulent spatial setting. Immediately upon Irma's appearance, however, this two-someness, this acting in concert, abruptly vanishes. The wife, or the family, is not mentioned again. The dreamer is suddenly *alone* with his worries, vis-à-vis a complaining patient. The visual field shrinks" (*DS*, 32). Thus, to be with Irma, to be confronted with Irma's pain, is for Freud, in Erikson's view, to be "*alone* with his worries" (Erikson's emphasis).

Lacan, on the other hand, in disputation—it must be conceded—of Erikson's overemphasis on the "we" in "we were receiving," affords us a symmetrical counterstatement: "The dear *Frau Doktor* remains absolutely invisible in the dream. One does not see her, she does not become [visually] apparent, not even for a single minute" (2:184).

It seems to me, however, that the real question, the real unsettling ambiguity and complexity of the feminine predicament in the dream, can only be understood, not through a separate examination of the female patient or of the wife, but through a synchronic *structural perception* of the symbolic *interaction* between the two: a structural perception that the dream invites through the substitutive movement and the visual condensation it effects. The dream seems to be asking: What is the meaning of the substitution? What is the *question* behind the condensation? What is the significance of the unconscious work (dream work) of tying Irma with the wife?

The Subject of Complaint

It is, indeed, as an agent of resistance and as a *subject of complaint* that the wife emerges from behind the female patient: as a subject, more specifically, of a rhetorically repressed complaint whose centrality is relegated to the paradoxically crucial marginality of a footnote: a footnoted feminine complaint whose centrality, in other words, is entrusted to a space peripheral to the text's consciousness, eccentric to its central argument.

But this is where, precisely, the creative writing of the dream occurs: off-center, in the margins.

> The still unexplained complaint of *pains in the abdomen* could also be traced back to this third figure. The person in question was, of course, my own wife; the pains in the abdomen reminded me of one of the occasions on which I had noticed her bashfulness. I was forced to admit to myself that I was not treating either Irma or my wife very kindly in this dream; but it should be observed by way of excuse that I was measuring them by the standard of the good and amenable patient. (110)

If, indeed, the still unexplained complaint of "pains in the abdomen" can be traced back from Irma to the wife, explicitly evoking the wife's sexual reticence or "bashfulness" in her husband's presence but implicitly also evoking—it might be assumed—the wife's rhetorically suppressed, unmentioned, silenced but protuberant pregnant condition, the scenario that the dream seems to unfold is that of the contamination, of the dynamic interpenetration, of different (differing) feminine complaints. Since, out of the footnote, the wife emerges as *a secret sharer in the feminine complaint* of the hysteric, the feminine complaint as such unfolds as more complex than it first seemed, in that it now appears to be articulated from different vantage points, from different structural positions.

What Do Women Want?

To understand the structural, and not just the thematic, implications of this feminine complaint, it is important to outline and keep in view at once the similarities and the *dis*similarities between the wife and Irma. It is from the dynamic play between the similarities and the dissimilarities that the full scope of the complaint emerges.

A. Obvious Similarities

1. The wife, like Irma, does not measure up to "the standard of the good and amenable patient." Both are resistant, recalcitrant to treatment. Speaking of his wife, as yet unnamed, Freud says, in the course of the associations: "She again was not one of my patients, nor should I have liked to have her as a patient, since I had noticed that she was bashful in my presence, and I could not think she would make an amenable patient" (4:110).

2. Irma has been infected, "infiltrated" by a male intervention: the injection of a "solution" from an unclean syringe. Metaphorically, the wife has been impregnated, fecundated by another male injection of another contaminating male solution.

B. Obvious Dissimilarities

1. "Irma's pains could be satisfactorily explained by her widowhood" (4:152). The complaint is coincident with the absence of a husband, in Irma's case, but with the presence of a husband, in the wife's case.

2. Freud's (pregnant) wife embodies female fertility. The hysteric patient embodies female sterility: that is why she is said to be, etymologically, "hysteric": "suffering from the womb."

C. *Paradoxical Similarities* (despite the Dissimilarities)

Both the sterile hysteric (widowed) and the pregnant wife (husbanded, happily married) are *suffering from the womb:* "The still unexplained complaint about *pains in the abdomen* could also be traced back"—from Irma to the wife (4:110).

D. *Paradoxical Implications of the Interpenetration of Complaints*

According to the patriarchal criteria, Freud's wife, beloved by her husband and pregnant with his child, is the social epitome of the *fulfilled woman.* Irma, on the other hand, as the widowed hysteric deprived of child and husband, is the social epitome of the *unfulfilled woman.* And yet, the dream is saying that *both women are unhappy,* lacking something. The dream unwittingly renders suspicious what we have come to call, today, "the feminine mystique," which consciously still governs Freud's, and his time's, views. But the way in which the feminine complaints are structured in the dream precisely puts in question the conventional idea of feminine fulfillment. Notwithstanding Freud's own consciousness and cultural beliefs, the dream suggests that the patriarchal myth of feminine fulfillment *could be* but a masculine wish fulfillment.

Whereas apparently, the wife's position as a woman is at the antipodes of that of Irma, the dream's creative work seems to belie this reassuring difference, to situate the two female positions as equivalent—exchangeable and interchangeable—in an equation of complaints whose *unknown* (the very riddle of femininity) calls, precisely, for a new articulation of the question: of the question of what Freud is up against in his professional and personal male encounter with femininity; of the question of how this encounter misses, or pragmatically subverts, all known answers given in advance; of the question of what Freud is up against in his encounter with the enigma of these women who should by now be known, and yet are still somehow, somewhere along the line, quite crucially unknown, unreadable, misunderstood, miscured, dissatisfied; of the question of what Freud is up against when the dream is telling him that the woman in his bed is as unknown, perhaps, and as dissatisfied, as the untalkative patient in his office, hysterically and painfully choking on a speech she cannot yield. In dramatizing femininity as an equation of diametrically opposed structural complaints leveled by the paradoxical common denominator of feminine dissatisfaction, the dream seems to be asking: where does the feminine desire really lie? My wife is "bashful in my presence"—what is it that my mate, my sexual partner, and the mother of my children truly wants? Irma resists my treatment—what is it that the patient truly wants? Is there a difference between female wish fulfillment and male wish-fulfilling fantasies of female wish fulfillment? Is there a difference between what a woman wants and what a man might think a woman wants? Where, exactly, does this difference lie? *What does a woman want?*

The entire dream is up against this question, which its unconscious, searching energy endeavors to articulate, through and beyond its own male plea.

The Wish Fulfillment of the Condensation

And yet, in asking, "What do women want?"—in going back and forth between the male plea and the feminine complaint, in not laying to rest the self-analytic dialogue between the two which constitutes the dream's own self-division—what is it that Freud wants? *What does the dreamer want?*

He does not simply want to overcome, to forcefully *reduce* female resistance and to stifle the complaint: he wants to *understand* it so that he can *answer* it appropriately, relieve the suffering. Freud's fundamental male wish is to *satisfy* each of these women: to satisfy the female wish. And yet, the dream is saying that he does not satisfy it: in all his various, varying male roles—as a husband, as a therapist, as a scientist, as an interpreter—Freud feels that he falls just short of giving satisfaction. As a husband, as a doctor, as a theoretician, Freud is up against feminine dissatisfaction.

And perhaps the wish fulfillment that the dream narcissistically accomplishes resides, precisely, in this very dreamlike condensation, in this very structure of exchangeability between the patient and the wife. What, indeed, if the dream's wish is ultimately to exchange the structural positions of wife and patient, to substitute the wife for Irma and Irma for the wife so as to *invert*, precisely, what the dreamer gets and does not get from each? In a way, what Freud wants from his wife is what he gets from Irma, but he also wants from Irma what he gets, precisely, from his wife.

What does Irma give him? Paradoxically enough, Irma gives him—a *complaint*, (the complaint of a patient to a doctor): that is, she gives him a speech act that actively solicits him, asks something of him; she *addresses him with her desire* (for relief). Irma demands him, calls him. But—she refuses to take in the seed of his "solution" and to be therapeutically fecundated by it.

On the other hand, his wife takes in his seed, gives him a child, but, "bashful in his presence," she shies away from him, *she does not address him with her desire.*

But the condensation opens up the wishful thinking (dreaming) of the possible exchange of the positions of these female gifts. Now, from his wife, Freud wants precisely the solicitation, the demand with which Irma appeals to him, addresses him. From Irma he desires, on the other hand, the opening and the fecundity of the wife: that is, it is with Irma, with the female patient, that he wishes, above all, to *give birth:* to *conceive psychoanalysis,* to procreate unprecedented insight, to give birth to a revolutionary (practical and theoretical) discovery.

This oneiric, wish-fulfilling structure of exchange between the female patient and the wife is itself, perhaps, embodied and condensed in the mediating figure of the third feminine persona of the dream: Irma's friend, whom Freud dreams up, precisely, as the phantasmically ideal woman patient, who "would have opened up her mouth" and "would have told him more than Irma." Through her, the dream's wish seems to be to understand women's unconscious (to have it open up to him) and to create, with women, through this unprecedented mode of therapeutic (human) partnership, an unprecedented mode of human (sexual) discourse, and an unprecedented mode of human (analytic, and analytically procreative) intercourse.

The Procreation of Psychoanalysis: The Pregnancy of the "Irma Dream"

In the most profound sense, the Irma dream is thus a *dream of pregnancy*, in all the repercussions of the word. In the most profound sense, it is a dream about the relation between difference and creation, between intercourse (all sorts of intercourse) and procreation (different modes of procreation). The dream is one of pregnancy, indeed, in a whole variety of ways: (1) it is pregnant with *the pregnancy of dreams;* (2) it is, most fundamentally, *pregnant with psychoanalysis* as a revolutionary practical and theoretical discovery; (3) it is pregnant, thus, with *Freud's own metaphoric pregnancy* of his new insight; (4) it is also pregnant, at the same time, with the *actual historic pregnancy of Freud's wife*, with which Freud's own creative pregnancy at once conflicts, competes, and tries to come to terms.

Since Freud's wife, however, happens to be pregnant with none other than Anna Freud, she is, in effect, *pregnant with a future to psychoanalysis*, which Freud does not yet dream of. Paradoxically enough, the wife is also pregnant with (a displacement of) what Freud does dream of: *an ideal female partner*. It would be tempting to continue dreaming about this interpenetration (inter-impregnation) of Freud's reality and Freud's dreams. History could not have better dreamed—or better written—the complex text of this incredible coincidence of pregnancies.

The recognition that the Irma dream is basically about conception—about the joint conception of Freud's child and of

Freud's nascent science—is indebted, it should be remembered, to Erikson's interpretation. However, notwithstanding the inspiring illumination that I think this Eriksonian insight brings into the dream, my own analysis of the meaning of Freud's conception, and of the original implications of the very pregnancy of the dream, is at variance with that of Erikson in a crucial way.

For in Erikson's view, it should be remembered, the dream's wishful conception of psychoanalysis is dreamed, primarily, as a *male conception:* as against the problematic background of his wife's conception of his child, Freud's wish is to conceive psychoanalysis with Fliess. "That a man," writes Erikson, "may incorporate another man's spirit," "that a man may conceive from another man, and that a man may be reborn from another, these ideas are the content of many fantasies and rituals which mark significant moments of male initiation, conversion and inspiration; and every act of creation, at one stage, implies the unconscious fantasy of inspiration by a fertilizing agent of a more or less deified, more or less personified mind or spirit" (*DS* 48).

Although I think this is a brilliant insight into the motive of pregnancy in the dream, and although I basically agree that Freud's homosexual attachment to the intellectual fecundity he gets from Fliess is doubtless built into the dream, I have suggested, for my part, that Freud's own wishful pregnancy is radically tied up with the dream's knot of female figures and that, rather than oneirically eliminating this knot so as to conceive psychoanalysis from Fliess, that is, to conceive psychoanalysis with no [female] resistance, through the wishful elimination of all [sexual] difference, the dream's wish is, precisely (but also most crucially), *to conceive psychoanalysis from the female patient.* What difference does that make with respect to that which is conceived, that which is specifically at stake in the conception?

In keeping with his view of "male initiation . . . and inspiration," Erikson conceives of Freud's conception as a primarily *conceptual* conception:

We will then appreciate another double meaning in the dream, which seems to speak for the assumption that one link between the medical, the intellectual, and the sexual themes of the dream is that of "conception." . . . The dreamer's worries concerning the growth of his family at this critical time of his professional life are clearly expressed in his letters to Fliess. At the same time, the typical association between biological *conception* and intellectual *concept formation* can be seen in the repeated reference to "germinating ideas." (*DS* 27, Erikson's emphasis)

What, however, does the Irma dream give birth to? With Fliess, Freud conceives, indeed, new concepts. But the Irma dream precisely dramatizes the sterility, the inefficacy of concepts: the sterility of theoretical "solutions" in practical dealings with the patient. What emerges in the Irma dream as absolutely crucial is the recognition that fecundity—psychoanalytical fecundity—is *not conceptual:* the patient has to "*accept* the solution," that is, not just to integrate, but to participate in, the conception of the insight. The doctor is no longer *master*—of the cure or of the patient, of the illness or of the "solution" to the illness. The analytical fecundity proceeds, precisely, from the doctor's destitution from his mastery (this is what the Irma dream is all about)—from the *destitution*, in effect, *of mastery as such.* The doctor is creative (pro-creative) only insofar as he is himself a subject of complaint, that is, only insofar as he is himself a patient: Irma's symptom in the shoulder is Freud's own. The subject of the dream is saying: I am myself a patient, a hysteric; I am myself creative only insofar as I can find a locus of fecundity in my own suffering. And I am procreative only insofar as I am not the master of that which I conceive, to the extent that I do not control what I give birth to. The doctor thus (fruitfully) communicates with the patient not by virtue of his opposition to, or difference from, the patient but by virtue of his own self-difference from himself: doctor and patient are both self-divided, and they communicate through their self-division.

In this way, indeed, the dream disrupts, and breaks away from, the patriarchal medical frame that structures it and still conditions its narration. The dream is saying that for Freud to give birth to psychoanalysis, the patient—bearing his own symptom—has first to give birth to herself: to her own therapy, to her own truth. And this is what the new discovery—the new fecundity—is all about.

To conceive psychoanalysis from Irma is thus an altogether different thing than to conceive psychoanalysis from Fliess. And the pregnancy of the Irma dream is pregnant with something new only insofar as it is *pregnant with this difference.* If, unlike Erikson, the dreamer knows it is impossible to do away with, to give birth without, the female patient, it is because psychoanalysis is here *conceived* (and this is the discovery the dream is pregnant with) less as a new "solution" (a new science, a new theory) than as a radically *new praxis of relating,* and as a radically *new praxis of relating theory and practice:* "solutions" and their dialogic procreation.

The Navel of the Dream

In the *conceptual male dream* of Freud and Fliess—a male dream Erikson so well translates—Irma can be said to be something like an irreducible female navel:

> There is [writes Freud] at least one spot in every dream at which it is unplumbable—a navel, as it were, that is its point of contact with the unknown. (4:111)

The figure of the navel is itself curiously related to the theme of pregnancy, both semantically (because of its metaphorical suggestiveness of the umbilical cord) and syntactically (because of its location in the text). Emerging, like Freud's wife, in the central marginality of a footnote: of the very footnote following, indeed, the one in which Freud's wife is mentioned (in connection with "the still unexplained complaint about *pains in the abdomen*"), the navel has two important levels of connotation: it functions, on the one hand, *theoretically,* as a new concept forged by Freud in order to denominate, to focalize abstractly, a whole framework of ideas relating to the *dream's resistance to understanding.* But on the other hand, it functions not abstractly but *concretely* (mobilizing the singularity of an image rather than the generality of a concept) in materially evoking a part of the human body which, located in the abdomen, could suggestively refer to the contiguous, though elliptical, suppressed) image of a pregnant belly. Could the navel of the dream and the navel of Freud's pregnant wife somehow communicate with respect to what the dream is pregnant with?

Why, indeed, does Freud choose to call "navel" the dream's relationship to the unknown? The navel marks the place where the umbilical cord is first attached and then (during delivery) cut off; it marks, in other words, at once the *disconnection* and the *connection* between a maternal body giving birth and a newborn child. The navel of the dream embodies, thus, the way in which the dream is, all at once, *tied up* with the unknown and *disconnected* from its knowledge, disconnected from the knowledge of its own begetting.

And yet, the disconnection has itself the form of a *knot:* the "navel" weaves into the theory of dreams the fundamental paradox of a *knotted disconnection that, itself, will never be untied.* Thus it is reformulated in the final chapter of Freud's book, no longer as a passing footnote but as a central theoretical conclusion:

> There is often a passage in even the most thoroughly interpreted dream which has to be left obscure; this is because we become aware during the work of interpretation that *at that point there is a tangle* of dream-thoughts *which cannot be unraveled* and which moreover adds nothing to our knowledge of the content of the dream. This is the dream's navel, the spot where it reaches down into the unknown. The dream-thoughts to which we are led by interpretation *cannot*, from the nature of things, *have any definite endings*, they are bound to *branch out in every direction into the intricate network* of our world of thought. It is at some point where this *meshwork* is particularly close that the dream-wish grows up, like a mushroom out of its mycelium. (4:525)

If the navel is a knot, it is not surprising that it is, precisely, *out of the very knot of female figures* that the notion of the navel for the first time springs, as a footnote to the Irma dream. "Thus," writes Freud,

> I had been comparing my patient Irma with two other people who would also have been recalcitrant to treatment. . . . For Irma

seemed to me foolish because she had not accepted my solution. Her friend would have been wiser. . . . She would have *opened her mouth properly*, and would have told me more than Irma. (4:111)

The crucial footnote follows:

I had a feeling that the interpretation of this part of the dream was not carried far enough to make it possible to follow the whole of its concealed meaning. If I had pursued *my comparison between the three women*, it would have taken me far afield.—There is at least one spot in every dream at which it is unplumbable—*a navel*, as it were, that is its point of contact with the unknown. (4:111, note 1)

Through the connection/disconnection of the dash ("it would have taken me far afield.—There is at least one spot in every dream . . ."), the navel of the Irma dream is here defined, it seems, as the "unplumbable" cluster of ("comparison between") the women. The question is, however, in what way can this equation of unknowns shed further light on what is happening in, and is begotten by, the specimen dream?

It is significant, of course, that the "unknown" is here emerging with a distinctly female connotation, and that the mystery of femininity (the tie among the women) and the mystery of the unknown ("the navel of the dream") are placed in the same structural position: the "spot where the dream reaches down into the unknown" seems to hinge on the unknowability of women. But what, precisely, does that mean? In what way is the "unknown" gender related?

Erikson suggests that the introduction of the image of "the navel of the dream" indicates that for Freud, "the Dream . . . is just another haughty woman, wrapped up in too many mystifying covers and 'putting on airs' like a Victorian lady." "In the last analysis," Erikson concludes, "the dream itself may be a mother image; she is the one, as the Bible would say, to be 'known'" (*DS*, 46).

It is no doubt true that the image of the navel is connected to the image of a mother and that, through the dream's complex of pregnancies, the wife as mother and, perhaps, the mother (or a mother) as a wife imbue the dream's unconscious thoughts and rhetorically affect, determine, and participate in the riddle of the female knot. It is equally quite pertinent to point out the link interconnecting epistemological and carnal knowledge, and to suggest, along with Erikson, that "in the last analysis . . . she [the Mother] is the one, as the Bible would say, to be 'known.'"

But can the *unknown* be simply reduced to, or defined by, that "which would be 'known'"? Can the unknown be subsumed by what we *know* we *cannot know*, and know, moreover, why? Can the *question* that the dream articulates as the unknowability of women be, indeed, subsumed by an *answer* (an immediate "male solution") that satisfactorily accounts for it: interprets the unknown away? Is not the tie among the women (the question of the dream's knot/navel) tied up, precisely, with the way in which male explanations guided by male expectations—the unilateral perspective of male desire—*does not* account for it?

In speaking of the navel as "unplumbable"—a *knot* ("a tangle of dream thoughts") which "cannot be unraveled", the dream interpreter is explicitly suggesting that the navel of the Irma dream, though hinging on the mystery of femininity, is by no means *a* woman (Mother, Victorian lady, Irma, and so forth) but the cluster of ("comparison between") the women, that is, a *structured female knot* that cannot be untied, a knot of female differentiality with respect to any given definition; a knot, in other words, which points not to the identifiability of any given feminine identity but to the inexhaustibility, the unaccountability, of *female difference:* difference that Freud—as man, as doctor, as interpreter—stumbles on, experiences at first as purely negative resistance, but which he then insightfully associates with the inexhaustibility, the unaccountability of the very *nodal point*—the very navel—of the dream.

Now, to explain female resistance, as well as the resistance of the navel of the dream, either by the generality of the incest prohibition or by the historical idiosyncrasy of Victorian prudery, is to *explain away* female resistance, to identify female resistance with male desire, and to erase the (sexual) difference between the two. But the Irma dream does not do that; or if it does that in the guise of its avowed male *wish fulfillment,* it does not do *just* that; it also writes, inscribes, the difference it erases; it also writes, inscribes, along with the discovery of wish fulfillment, the historical discovery of the *pregnancy of the difference* that its wish fulfillment narcissistically erases.

What cannot be overemphasized, it seems to me, in Freud's dream theory, is the fact, and the significance of the fact, that the theoretical emergence of the notion of wish fulfillment is coincident with the theoretical emergence of the notion of the navel, which is its truly revolutionary counterpart. The very birth, indeed, of the concept of the navel of the dream in the place of the oneirically wish-fulfilling male erasure of ("male solution" to) female difference bears witness to Freud's insight that *to solve the riddle is to fail to account for the question of the dream.*

What is, then, the question that the dream discovers, the question that the specimen dream is quite literally *engrossed with?* Is there a different, nonreductive way in which the unknown, the dream's navel, can be, not accounted for, explained away, subsumed by what is known, but rather thought out as the way in which the genuine unknown of gender and of gender difference—the radical unknown of sexuality as difference—*fecundates* at once Freud's dream and the unprecedented theory to which the dream historically gives birth?

To Dream a Question

The navel of the Irma dream is constituted, we have seen, by the unfathomability, the inexhaustibility, of the comparison of the three resistant women. But there is a paradox in the way the navel knots its own unknowability. For the dream interpreter is saying that this knot of women is, as such, "unplumbable," not because it simply is unknowable, but insofar as its very unknowability constitutes, paradoxically enough, the dream's specific *"point of contact with the unknown"* (4:111). The dream, in other words, through the resistance of the women, *makes contact* here with something new, something that it does not know or understand or master but with which it nonetheless somehow communicates. Can we try to situate in the text what it is the Irma dream makes contact with at this specific moment? Can the dream in any way shed light on what the disconnection paradoxically connects with?

At the specific textual point where the navel footnote in effect cuts off the interpretive flow of the associations ("There is at least one spot in every dream at which it is unplumbable"), the text thus interrupted by the footnote has, in comparing the three women, just touched upon—connected with—an image: the image of a female throat. "She [Irma's friend] would have opened her mouth properly, and would have told me more than Irma." (Footnote: "I had a feeling that the interpretation of this part of the dream was not carried far enough to make it possible to follow the whole of its concealed meaning. If I had pursued my comparison between the three women, it would have taken me far afield.—There is at least one spot in every dream at which it is unplumbable, a navel, as it were, that is its point of contact with the unknown.") In Freud's text, the quotation of the dream's text follows: "*What I saw in her throat: a white patch* . . ." Can this connection with the throat somehow shed light on the connection/disconnection of the navel?

The signifier of the throat may lead the reader of Freud's text in two directions: on the one hand, the ensuing vision of the female throat—the oneiric, horrifying confrontation with the unknown of an opened female cavity—leads, in the dream's narrative, to the male/medical diagnosis linked to the injection of a male solution. But on the other hand, the throat may be associated not just with the (wish-fulfilling) male solution but also with the initial feminine complaint. "If you only knew," Irma said to Freud, "what pains *I've got now in my throat* and stomach and abdomen—it's choking me." The word in the German original for the way her painful throat is strangling her is *zusammenschnüren*, which literally reads: "*it's tying me up in knots.*"

The Knot in Irma's Throat

The *female knot* that constitutes the *nodal point* of the Irma dream—the dream's knot/navel—is thus prefigured in the initial image of the *painful knot*—the lump in Irma's throat—which somehow triggers, opens up, the self-divided, self-analytic dialogue of Freud's dream.

In a way, it could be said that *Freud's whole dream precisely speaks out of the lump in Irma's throat.* It is out of a knot of female pain that Freud's dream issues: a dream about a knot of female pain recalcitrant to, and in excess of, Freud's discourse (Freud's interpretation); a dream about a knot of irreducibly resistant women; a dream about a knot of feminine complaints.

The dream is painful, encompassing both Freud's and Irma's pain, and measuring the irreducible discrepancy between the two. But there is an insight, a discovery, in the very pain of this discrepancy.

From the singularly silent and resistant navel of Freud's pregnant wife, to the singularly painful and resistant knot in Irma's throat, through the mediating notion of the navel of the dream, Freud discovers that resistance, far from being simply negative, is a positively pregnant concept; that resistance is a textual knot, a nodal point of unknown significance, the navel of an unknown text; and that the psychoanalytic dialogue is a new way of reading, and of working with, the pregnancy of this unknown and the fecundity of this resistance. This is what the Irma dream makes contact with, precisely, through the navel of its female knot ("a navel, as it were, that is its point of contact with the unknown") but what the dreamer and the dream interpreter *do not yet know.*

Freud discovers, thus, as yet unconsciously, *the very origin of self-analysis,* the very motivating force of analytic dialogue, in the oneirically unfolded navel of sexuality as difference: of sexuality as the ungraspable, intuited relation between the navel of a "bashful" pregnant belly and the choking, strangling knot of pain in Irma's throat. As the ungraspable foundation of a radical unconscious dramatized by the complex, dramatic figure of the pregnant navel/knot in Irma's throat, sexuality is, in the Irma dream, envisioned as a double reference—a connection/disconnection—on the one hand, to the body, and on the other hand, to speech. Human sexuality, in other words, is here (self-analytically) envisioned on the one hand as a *differentiality of pain* and on the other hand as *the unspeakability of difference:* as an irreducible *bodily gap in language* (an irreducible hole in a borrowed kettle).

In much the same way as the navel of the dream, the knot of pain that ties up Irma's throat remains, indeed, eccentric to Freud's speech and irreducibly resistant to interpretation (although the dream itself explains this female knot of pain as the differential, symptomatic *residue* of the injection of a *male solution*).

In recapitulating the resistance of the female knot—the knot of (the comparison between the) women—the female knot of pain in Irma's throat, which symbolizes at the same time Irma's pain and Irma's choking speech, embodies, thus, the very navel of the feminine complaint, and of the feminine complaint's resistance to interpretation: a knot that is at once the *nodal point* of the female pain and that which makes the nodal point of the female pain *unspeakable:* unspeakable in a male dream, unspeakable in terms of a male (self-conscious, self-identical) solution.

The genius of Freud's dream is to have recognized, precisely, that; and to have situated both the psychoanalytic lesson of the feminine resistance, and this unspeakability of the feminine complaint within his own male dream, this differentiality of the female knot of pain with respect to his own theoretical solutions as the very nodal point of his specimen dream and as, indeed, the very *navel* of his dream of understanding.

Because Freud's dream can think beyond its conscious means; because Freud's genius gives us insight even into its own limitations, the author/writer of the Irma dream, in grappling with the female knots of his own text and in theorizing the pathbreaking notion of the navel of the dream, has nonetheless given us some textual access into the unknown. Freud calls precisely "navel" this textual access that he does not command and whose meaning he is not entirely in possession of.

The "navel" is, in other words, Freud's discovery—through the Irma dream—that in every theory, interpretation, or conscious meaning there is a disconnection: that in every thought there is the navel of a dream; but also, that in every dream there is the navel of a thought. Whether the textual access that the navel gives us into the unknown is drifting us from dream to thought or from thought to dream is what remains to be determined at any given moment, and what is often undecidable. The visionary thinking power of the dream from which psychoanalysis proceeds resides, however, in the groundbreaking ways in which the dream's knot/navel knots together—for the whole future of psychoanalysis—the question of the navel and the question of the woman as *resistance*.

The dreamer is predicting here, in other words, that femininity—the question of the woman and the woman as a question—is bound to remain unsolved and unresolved in psychoanalytic theory to the extent, precisely, that it is the very *navel of psychoanalysis:* a nodal point of significant resistance in the text of the ongoing psychoanalytic dream of understanding; a navel that, although "unplumbable," is also positively (to borrow once again Freud's terms) psychoanalysis's "point of contact with the unknown": psychoanalysis's potential for renewal, for a renewed discovery of its own special, revolutionary insight, through its continuing dynamic play—and self-analytic dialogue—with the unconscious of its own self-difference.

5

With Whom Do You Believe Your Lot Is Cast?

Woolf, de Beauvoir, Rich, and the Struggle for Autobiography

(Afterword)

> I felt a Cleaving in my mind
> As if my Brain had split—
> I tried to match it—Seam by Seam—
> But could not make them fit.
>
> The thought behind, I strove to join
> Unto the thought before
> But Sequence ravelled out of Sound
> Like Balls—upon a floor.
>
> —EMILY DICKINSON

I

Another Story, or the Performativity of Understanding

At the end of chapter 1, I wrote: "If the critical suggestion I am making in this book is that people tell their stories (which they do not know or cannot speak) through others' stories, then the very force of insight of this critical suggestion was at once born out and actively enacted, put in motion, by the process of my writing, which was *driven*, in effect, by the ways in which I was precisely missing my own implication in the texts before me."

What is there to say, now, beyond the analysis of psychoanalysis? In what way did I unwittingly again tell another story through Freud's story, and how did I, once more, miss something crucial of my own autobiography in it?

In contrast to the writing of the other chapters, I was, in fact, partially aware, even while I wrote the chapter on psychoanalysis (chapter 4), of its causal connection to my life. And yet, this known connection implicated, at the same time, an important disconnection (I was writing about Freud's discovery "that in every theory, interpretation or conscious meaning there is a disconnection")—a disconnection that continued to escape me.

I was at the time myself in psychoanalysis with a male analyst. Specifically, the Freud chapter was written under the impact of the successful practical analysis of one or two of my own dreams, a practical analysis that revealed to me, uncannily, my own life story as unknown—that is, not merely unrecognized but unsuspected. The unique persuasiveness and the amazing findings of this actual process of association and interpretation in the psychoanalytic setting carried overwhelming proofs of the radical difference between any conceivable theoretical understanding of those dreams (any academic exercise of interpretation) and the uncanny force of act of this performativity of understanding. From this experience, I learned how dreams are indeed, concretely and materially, the "royal road to the unconscious," how they were susceptible of telling us *about our own autobiography another story* than the one we knew or had believed to be our own, delivering a different kind of evidence and transmitting, thus, a narrative that cannot be narrated, or even imagined, in any other way.

The insights gained into my own autobiography—and into my own ignorance of it—drove me to look closely at the way in which Freud's theory implies, in fact, a *revolution* in the very *theory of autobiography*, and at the way in which, in writing down his new theory of dreams, *Freud was writing in effect his own autobiography* (*The Interpretation of Dreams*).

What I did not know then was how the chapter on a revolutionary *male* autobiography was in effect already pointing to the present thought and to the present theory on *female* autobiography, and how the analysis of Freud's autobiography would later lead me to rethink, and wonder at, the altogether different questions raised by the autobiographical attempts of women. What I did not know, in other words, was how the longing that the Freud chapter was unwittingly inscribing to address "the-man-who-would-understand,"[1] ideally a man whose capacity of insight and of innovation would equal Freud's, was in effect a secret, deeper longing to address profoundly the autobiography of women (including my own) and to appeal to, or to be in touch with, the community of women through the common questions of the difficulty—the impossibility—of their autobiography.

The male clinician who was my companion in this psycho-analytic journey was a caring listener, an insightful guide, and an enabling catalyst. Yet I felt that he might well have failed to understand, or to take into account, something crucial about me as a woman, thus someone in a different position than himself. I also felt that he had no warning of this something he was missing, since neither psychoanalytic theory nor his clinical training had prepared him for it, even though they enabled him effectively to understand me in other ways (to enable me to understand myself, and to see me through this journey).

Once I tried, during a session, to discuss feminism with him, so as to alert him to the necessity of not taking for granted common-places about women, but after listening for a few minutes, he closed this topic off by saying: "It's *your* time: *you are paying* for it." He had a point: I was sounding like a lecture, I was "intellec-tualizing." Yet I felt that something very crucial could not be said, and thus remained unheard, did not get articulated. I wrote the essay on Freud as an attempt precisely to articulate this unarticu-lated; the writing was implicitly addressed to him, in the hope that it would make him understand, or at least make an allowance for, something that he did not understand and that had to do both with his difference of position and with the limits of his theory, which erased that difference and was not even alert to the erasure.

And indeed, it was my time. And I was paying. And I was running out of psychoanalytic time. I felt, however, that with regard to my female destiny and to the costly implications of my gender, there remained a debt that was unpaid, perhaps unpayable. It is to pay this debt that I engaged in a reflection about Freud's destiny as a creative thinker and as a male therapist of women: to pay a debt to the real efficacy of psychoanalysis as a new and unprecedented way of listening; but also to acknowledge what remains unpayable, in psychoanalytic terms, with respect to what, and how, women are paying.

That much I knew. What I did not know, or did not clearly see, was how this chapter, like its predecessors, was again a testimony to the way in which my own autobiography was as yet missing, because I still could not essentially address it to myself—truly address it, that is, to a woman.

Structures of Address

As opposed to the two chapters on Balzac (whose structure of address is less defined), the Freud chapter was thus prompted by the original (historical) desire to be understood by—and to reach an understanding with—a man. Did I betray the feminist perspective—and my feminist commitment—by this desire? I did not think so at the time, and for different reasons, I still do not believe today (as some others do, or might) that the touchstone of feminist integrity and the condition of feminist loyalty rest in a concerted censorship of any form of address to men. At the point where I am today, however, I have become much more acutely conscious of the necessity of underscoring the address to women and of specifically avoiding, and explicitly decentering, any inadvertent semblance of a male-centered structure of address.

At the time I wrote the chapter, I wanted to include both men and women in my address. If I destined my ideas and the process of my thinking to, among others, an implicit privileged male reader, it was because my effort then was precisely to *include* men in the feminist critique of their position. My main concern in the writing was then to elaborate an innovative *structure of address* that would be specifically *inclusive*, as opposed to the *exclusive* structure of address I was deciphering in Freud, and which I saw as typical of patriarchal utterances, which by definition—if sometimes unwittingly—erase women as subjects while maintaining their position as desired objects, always fascinating, sometimes baffling, at moments incomprehensible. I did not want to respond in sort: I did not want to exclude Freud, to erase men as potential addressees, and to repeat the patriarchal structure of exclusion in reverse; I wanted rather to attempt to transform this structure by making its exclusions patent and by performatively demonstrating their lack of integrity (in all senses of the word), by interposing my own voice as a woman reader inside Freud's utterance, and by thus enacting its rhetorical and philosophical explosion from its own inside.

My perspective in the chapter on Freud was thus similar to the one Carol Gilligan defines, from her different vantage point as a clinical psychologist and sociologist, in her innovative study of adolescent girls. "In these struggles over connection," writes Gilligan about those adolescents, "I saw evidence of a central dilemma of inclusion: how to include both oneself and others." Women, observes Gilligan, often have recourse to the strategy of excluding themselves for the sake of others, so as to live up to the idealizing but self-serving patriarchal image of femininity—or womanlihood—as sheer nurturance and utter selflessness. But as every therapist is well aware, this strategy is doomed to fail. However, to repair relationships by excluding others does not provide a viable solution, either. "Adolescence," Gilligan sums up, "poses problems of connection for girls coming of age in Western culture":

> Girls are tempted or encouraged to solve these problems by excluding themselves or by excluding others—that is, by being a good woman, or by being selfish. Many current books advocate

one or the other of these solutions. Yet the problem girls face in adolescence is also a problem in the world at this time: the need to find ways of making connection in the face of difference.[2]

The need to find ways of making connections in the face of difference—the need to stand the ground of the difference and yet to find ways to communicate and even to convey something of that difference across the gap it creates, the need to speak and to reach out—in speaking and in listening—*across (sexual and other) difference*, was thus the main original concern of the structure of address that directed, at the time of its conception, my study of Freud's dream.

Another Scene of Choices

Today, I still uphold the necessity of a *structure of address inclusive of its otherness*, but I have a slightly different view, and a different urgency, about who should be addressed and how to leave room for inclusion. The balance in my own structure of address has somewhat changed. And so has my conception of what is essentially, profoundly, involved in an address.

The need to speak to women without the intermediary of a man, to listen more attentively to women, and to address more urgently the community of women, has imposed itself as a corollary of my growing sense that the feminine predicament of "the absence of a story" (or its counterpart, "the presence of too many stories") can be truly grasped, and perhaps remedied, only through the bond of reading, only through a female sharing and exchange of stories; that only women can *empower* women's story *to become a story*, and that each woman's story can become a story only through women's collective perception of themselves. In a poem entitled, profoundly and provocatively, "There Are No Honest Poems about Dead Women," African American poet Audre Lorde asks:

> What do we want from each other
> after we have told our stories
> do we want

> to be healed   do we want
> mossy quiet stealing over our scars
> do we want
> the all-powerful unfrightening sister
> who will make the pain go away
> mother's voice   in the hallway
> . . . .
> I buy time with another story.[3]

Perhaps it could be said that the time we "buy" from men is not—or cannot be—"an honest poem" (in Audre Lorde's expression, "There are no honest poems about dead women"). It is from women that we must "buy time," and it is with women that we must, today, create time.

An address is not merely an act of intellectual and emotional appeal. It is an *act of empowerment*. And such empowerment becomes possible only when women can transmit and grasp—their own metaphoricity to one another, only when each woman can become (however different) the metaphor for another woman. To put it differently, the collective empowerment of women becomes possible only when, to borrow Carolyn Heilbrun's acute terms, "women no longer live their lives isolated in the houses and the stories of men,"[4] when woman is "dragged by the roots of her own will into another scene of choices."[5]

In this other scene of address and this *other scene of choices*, there emerges a new question that, in some ways, resonates to, echoes, answers, complements Freud's question "What does a woman want?" but in other ways displaces, deconstructs it:

> *With whom do you believe your lot is cast?*
> *From where does your strength come?*
>
> I think somehow, somewhere
> every poem of mine must repeat those questions
>
> which are not the same. There is a *whom*, a *where*
> that is not chosen   that is given   and sometimes falsely given[6]

Uttered in a poem by Adrienne Rich and reverberating, in effect, from one poem to another, from one book of poetry to another,[7] this other question which offsets Freud's question could perhaps be thought of as a female question:

> *With whom do you believe your lot is cast?*
> If there's a conscience in these hills
> it hurls that question
>
> unquenched, relentless, to our ears
> *wild and witchlike*
> ringing every swamp[8]

Perhaps this question in its turn implies Freud's question ("What does a woman want?"), but employing different pronouns (neither *I* nor *she* but *you*), thus defined in different terms, understood in different registers, no longer a "what" but a "with whom," its *desire* is, precisely, (unlike Freud's) a desire of *address* (*With whom do* you *believe* your lot *is cast?*), and its question is one of empowerment (*From where does your strength come?*).

Another Scene of Inclusion

The present chapter, thus, primarily addresses women. It is therefore not specifically addressed to men in explicit or direct ways. Yet I want to leave room for inclusion. I want not just to strive toward "a room of our own" but to strive toward the necessity of *making room*. What this means is that, ironically enough, I too (very like Virginia Woolf, who has been criticized for it), remain "acutely conscious" of the fact that while addressing women I am being "overheard" (and even heard) by men, and *I mean to be thus overheard and heard.* I take the risk of this inclusion—and of this acknowledgment—I take the chance (in all senses of the word) of this self-conscious affirmation, even though I am aware that it goes against the grain of what has nowadays become a commonplace in radical feminist perception, which considers this inclusiveness as a simple oversight on Woolf's part (something we can leave behind us in our quest for progress), an oversight deriving from Woolf's inadvertent fear of falling short of feminine "propriety" (the impossibility of appearing angry and remaining "feminine"). For this alleged impossibility of getting truly angry, Woolf is repeatedly reproached and criticized in the now famous terms first formulated by Adrienne Rich:

> In rereading Virginia Woolf's *A Room of One's Own* (1929) . . . I was astonished at the sense of effort, of pains taken, of dogged tentativeness, in the tone of that essay. . . . *Virginia Woolf is addressing an audience of women, but she is acutely conscious—as she always was—of being overheard by men:* By Morgan and Lytton and Maynard Keynes and for that matter by her father, Leslie Stephen. . . .
>
> No male writer has written primarily or even largely for women, or with the sense of women's criticism as a consideration, when he chooses his materials, his theme, his language. But to a lesser or greater extent, every woman writer has written for men even when, like Virginia Woolf, she was supposed to be addressing women. If we have come to *the point when this balance might begin to change*, when women can stop being haunted, . . . then it is an extraordinary moment for the woman writer—and reader.[9]

Looking back at my own chapters, I acknowledge I have reached, precisely in these very pages, "the point where the balance might begin to change" or has begun to change; the crucial point of the tipping, of the changing, of the balance. And it would be naive to presume that because of feminism such a change can be taken for granted or given in advance to any woman (to presume that we are already out of the cave and not coming out of it). Rich has a point, which she formulates, as always, with a forceful straightforwardness and with an incisive displacement of perspective that cannot but be, in effect, decisively illuminating.

But can the question of address be so summarily subsumed by a simple question of *polarized sexual identities?* Are our structures of address in reality so simple and so self-evidently clear-cut? Let me illustrate this question, and illustrate what I believe to be the infinite complexity of real structures of address, by quoting—and by looking at the questions raised by—the inaugural paragraph of Vita Sackville-West's autobiography, an autobiography that she felt compelled to lock up during her lifetime and which her son, who most probably was not its primary or most likely addressee, found (as an inadvertent part of his filial legacy) and published (inside the added frame of his own narrative) after her death. Although the material destiny of this autobiography is extraordinary, I will suggest its opening as metaphorical and as exemplary of the complexity unwittingly implicit in *any female autobiographical address.*

> Of course [writes Vita] *I have no right* whatsoever to write down the truth about my life, *involving as it naturally does the lives of so many other people*, but I do so *urged by a necessity of truth-telling*, because there is no living soul who knows the complete truth; here, may be one who knows a section; and there, one who knows another section: but to the whole picture not one is initiated. *Having written it down I shall be able to trust no one to read it; there is only one person in whom I shall have utter confidence that I would give every line of this confession into his hands*, knowing that after wading through this morass—for it is a morass, my life, a bog, a swamp, a deceitful country, with one bright patch in the middle, the patch that is unalterably his—I know that after wading through it all he would emerge holding his estimate of me steadfast. This would be the test of my confidence, from which I would not shrink. *I would not give it to* her—*perilous touchstone!, who* even in these first score of lines *should teach me where truth lies. I do know where it lies, but have no strength to grasp it;* here I am already in the middle of my infirmities.[10]

Vita is writing the story of her painful breakup with her female lover, Violet Treifusis, a rupture that the pressures of her marriage and her concrete attachment to her husband, Harold Nicolson, have compelled her to enact. The autobiography is primarily the story of a loss, of a radical split and splitting her life has undergone. The questions of address this opening enacts are many: Whom do we *write for?* Whom do we *wish* to be *read by?* Whom are we *afraid* to be read by? Whom do we *trust* to know how to read our writing? Whom do we need in order to *help us grasp the truth* that lies in wait (for us, for others) in our story but that alone we do not have the strength to grasp? Who can help us, or *enable us,* to *survive our story?* Who is our *internal witness?*[11] Who is our *external witness?* Who is our *voluntary* witness? Who is our *inadvertent* witness? The writing testifies not merely to the questions (ever so nuanced, multidimensional, and increasingly complex) but to the inherited dramatic conflicts that structure the potential answers and to the fact that the answers are neither self-transparent (in Vita's own mind) nor clear-cut (they do not coincide with their apparent, stated opposition). The questioning can thus proceed only through negation and self-negation and through a constant movement of displacement and self-displacement. "Having written it down I shall be able to trust no one to read it." And immediately, contradictorily: "there is only one person in whom I shall have utter confidence that I would give every line of this confession into his hands." Vita here alludes to her husband: she can only think of giving her autobiography to *him.* "I will not give it to *her*—perilous touchstone!, who even in this first score of lines should teach me where truth lies." Yet in effect, Vita has not given "it" to "him." She has written it, in spite of herself, for "her," or because of her, as every word of the autobiography bears witness to against itself, against its conscious, or self-conscious, or deliberate intention. She has written, in effect, an autobiography about the impossibility of giving her autobiography to her.

Who is, then, the real addressee of the autobiography? Is it the husband, Harold, the man who in her consciousness is the only one she can trust and who she hopes will understand her? Is it Violet, the woman she loves but from whom she felt compelled to separate herself because the truth this woman was a catalyst of was unbearable? Is it Virginia Woolf, who from a similar position of a beloved woman will listen to the story some ten years later? Is it Virginia not simply as another woman lover but as another *woman writer,* a woman writer to whom Vita has perhaps succeeded finally in giving her autobiography and who will answer it with her own public testimony in writing in her turn *Orlando* (*A Biography*), illustrated by the real photos of, and dedicated to, Vita Sackville-West?[12] Could the addressee be, on the other hand,

Vita's mother, from whom Vita had inherited the scheme (as well as the confusion and the anger) of patriarchal obligations and who might therefore be, in some obscure ways, at the origin of the story's silence (its self-censorship) as well as of the story's careless and uncomprehending repetition, when, in her senility, she leaks the story to her grandsons, Vita's children? "My grandmother disillusioned me, by unfolding the whole Violet story; explaining how my mother had been determined to desert her husband and the two little boys . . . ; how a few years later a second woman entered my mother's life and again almost wrecked the marriage. ('That Mrs. Woolf, who described in that book [*Orlando*] how your mother *changed her sex!*')" (181–82). Could the real address- ee of the autobiography be thus at once *its censor* and *its convention- al (mis)reader*, in the figure of the mother (or the grandmother) about whom Virginia Woolf would subsequently say: "The old woman ought to be shot!" (183)? Could the real addressee (how- ever inadvertent) be the son who, posthumously to his mother's life, finds the manuscript and, through its publication, *makes it public?* Or could the real addressees be, on the other hand, our- selves, posterity, its future readers? "Of course," wrote Vita, "I have no right whatsoever to write down the truth about my life, involving as it naturally does the lives of so many other people." The lives of other people are not merely "involved" in Vita's autobiography; they are what the autobiography is actively trying to *address*.

But as Vita's text (and real story) shows, and as Balzac's text (and fictitious story) demonstrates in yet another context (the story of what happens to Henri de Marsay in "The Girl with the Golden Eyes"), we do not always know who is *the real addressee* of the text of our desire and of the writing of our life. It is this impossibility of fully knowing and this constant search—this struggle for cognizance in regard to the vital, shifting possibilities of change in our structures of address—that is, precisely, what the story of the Other is telling us each time anew and what female autobiography, I would suggest, is striving, at its most profound, to narrate.

II

Bearing Witness

Reading autobiographically is, then, essentially an act of giving testimony: of giving testimony to the unsuspected, unexpected "feminine resistance" in the text (see chapter 1). Bearing witness is, however, crucially, a noncoercive act. It cannot be a question of forcing a text to say what is outside of it, or of imposing our own autobiography on literature. It cannot be a question of extrapolating feminism into the literary work, or of presuming in advance that the text will indeed comprise anything like a (textual) feminine resistance. We bear witness not to an expectation (ideological or autobiographical) but to a literary process of surprise, to the way in which the Other (and the story of the Other) has addressed us by surprising us, and has, in fact, surprised us all the more that its unexpected revelation—this "feminine resistance" in the text—has effectively, unwittingly, addressed some forces, some desires, some events in our own life.

Reading autobiographically cannot, therefore, be merely a question of encroaching, with one's own story, on the feminine resistance in the text. More demandingly and more attentively, it is a question of *experiencing this feminine resistance as a joint effect of interaction among literature, autobiography and theory,* insofar as all three modes *resist, precisely, one another.* It is utilizing theory, in other words, as *self-resistance.* It is engaging in a paradoxical attempt of reading literature and one's own life with the tools—and through the resources—of theory but, at the same time, reading literature and one's own life as, precisely, a *resistance to theory:*[13] using one's autobiography as a resistance to theory but, at the same time, just as crucially, using theory and literature as, precisely, a *resistance to autobiography.*

The most innovative women writers who have "authorized autobiography,"[14] those whom we regard as our "founding mothers," have authorized it only through such a resistance, a resistance all too quickly overlooked today but one that each of these women writers took pains to articulate and to inscribe in the very midst of her autobiographical endeavor.

"I have *hesitated* to do what I am going to do now, which is to use myself as an illustration," writes Adrienne Rich in her inaugural text, "When We Dead Awaken" (38), the text which has set up, indeed, the model (and the fashion) of the autobiographical, personal example. "For a long time," writes Simone de Beauvoir in the introduction to *The Second Sex*, "I have *hesitated* to write a book on woman" (vii). These *hesitations* are not simply overcome, erased, forgotten; they are inscribed, recorded, written permanently into the text. In the case of Rich, theory (the theory of "Writing as Re-Vision") hesitates to become autobiography (the personal example). In the case of de Beauvoir, autobiography (her own female destiny) hesitates to become theory (*The Second Sex*). But in both cases, what is at stake is not merely the combination of autobiography and theory but their interaction: not merely their mutual information but their mutual transformation. And in both cases, the *hesitation* itself (the clash between autobiography and theory as *self-resistance*) is both autobiographical and theoretical.

The Resistance to Autobiography: Adrienne Rich

From where? the voice asks coldly.

This is the voice in cold morning air
that pierces dreams. *From where does your strength come?*

—ADRIENNE RICH, "Sources"

In the "New Introduction" to her book entitled *Of Woman Born: Motherhood as Experience and Institution*, Rich makes a point of the theoretical, impersonal purpose of this mingling of autobiography with theory:

Of Woman Born was both praised and attacked for what was sometimes seen as its odd-fangled approach: *personal testimony mingled
with research*, and *theory which derived from both*. But this approach
never seemed odd to me in the writing. What still seems odd is the
absentee author, the writer who lays down speculations, theories,
facts, and fantasies without any personal grounding. On the other
hand, I have felt recently that the late 1960's Women's Liberation's thesis that "the personal is political" (which helped release
this book into being) has been laid by a New Age blur of the
personal-for-its-own-sake, as if "the personal is good" had become the corollary and the thesis forgotten.[15]

If "the personal" is indeed "political," it is not there simply for its
own sake: it is there for the sake of theory, of whose "re-vision" it
is a vehicle.

But Rich's *theory* is itself *resisted*, and exceeded, by her literary
art, by her poetry. "But poems are like dreams," she says herself in
"When We Dead Awaken": "In them you put what you don't
know you know" (40). In "Diving into the Wreck," a poem written under the impact of the cataclysm her life has undergone
through her separation from her husband, his tragic suicide, and
her own discovery of a hitherto unknown intensity of love in the
revelation of "one woman's meaning to another woman,"[16] Rich
herself *resists* and in effect subverts her own theory[17] about the
necessity for a woman writer to symmetrically reverse the patriarchal structure of address and to be strict about addressing wom-
en *as opposed to* addressing men. Her own poetic structure of
address is infinitely more complex than her theory, and it specifically explodes the symmetries of any pronominal (he/she) or
sexual (men/women) polarization:

> This is the place.
> And I am here, the mermaid whose dark hair
> streams black, the merman in his armored body
> We circle silently
> about the wreck
> we dive into the hold.
> *I am she: I am he* . . .

> *We are, I am, you are*
> by cowardice or courage
> the one who find our way back to this scene
> carrying a knife, a camera
> a book of myths
> in which
> our names do not appear.[18]

The poem underscores, indeed, both the difference that distinguishes and separates its project from a simple project of confession, and its radical *absence of story*, or *resistance* to a simple mode of *narrative:*

> I came to explore the wreck.
> The words are purposes.
> The words are maps.
>
> . . . .
>
> The thing I came for:
> *the wreck and not the story of the wreck*
> the thing itself and not the myth
> (23, my emphasis)

Rather than confess, the poetry bears witness:

> You, bearing ceaselessly
> yourself   the witness
>
> . . . .
>
> traveller and witness
> the passion of the speechless
> driving your speech
> protectless.[19]

To herself, to others, to the speechless, to her own autobiography, the poet is not just a witness, but a precocious witness:[20]

> The movement of the wrist does not change
> but the pen plows deeper
>
> *my handwriting flows into words*
> *I have not yet spoken*

> I'm the sole author of nothing
> the book moves from field to field
>
> of testimony   recording
> how the wounded teach each other. . .[21]
>
> . . . *these scars bear witness* . . .
>
> There where every wound is registered as
>   scar tissue . . .
>
> Go back so far there is another language
> go back far enough the language
> is no longer personal
>
> these scars bear witness[22]

The poetry is thus at once autobiography and resistance to auto-biography, at once a vehicle for theory and yet also a crucial vehicle for the resistance to theory, insofar as poetry "thinks through the body" and explores reality through fiction.[23] Yet, "to write poetry or fiction is not to fantasize," insists Rich,[24] in much the same way as Virginia Woolf, in turn, asserts, "fiction here is likely to contain more truth than fact."[25]

The Resistance to Autobiography: Simone de Beauvoir

> If I have held her at arm's length till now
> if I have still believed it was
> my loyalty, my punishment at stake
>
> If I dare imagine her surviving
> I must be fair to what she must have lived through
> I must allow her to be at last
>
> political in her ways   not in mine
> her urgencies perhaps   impervious to mine
> defining revolution as she defines it.
>
> —ADRIENNE RICH, "For Ethel Rosenberg"

It is a similar kind of interaction between theory, autobiography, and literature that is experienced, in a different culture and through a different "force of circumstance," by French philosopher and writer Simone de Beauvoir: an interaction between theory, autobiography, and literature that, for de Beauvoir, has constituted a precise itinerary: the very one that has led her to *The Second Sex*.

Wanting to talk about herself, de Beauvoir realizes that it is impossible to write a female autobiography without passing, first, through *theory*. Since the theory she needs is not yet in existence, she creates it, by researching and by synthesizing the two volumes of the groundbreaking insights of *The Second Sex*.

Only later does this theory in turn lead to the successive volumes of de Beauvoir's autobiography. Some of her readers will, however, argue that even in her memoirs the narrative does not get personal enough and that it is, in fact, only her literary writings that are truly autobiographical. Literature, autobiography, and theory remain, thus, to the end of her career, inextricably tied together in the way in which they mutually resist and yet mutually inhabit one another.

> I explained why . . . I decided to continue my autobiography. . . . From others as well as from myself, there was no lack of objections: "It's too soon." . . . "Wait until you can say everything." . . . And even: "After all, you reveal more of yourself in your novels." None of this is untrue. But I have no choice.
>
> In fact, I wanted to write about myself. I liked Leiris' *L'Age d'homme; such sacrificial essays, in which the author strips himself bare without excuses, appealed to me.*[26]

But this desire for confession is resisted by the irresistible emergence—and by the uncompromising rigor—of a theoretical necessity:

> I let the idea begin to take shape, made a few notes. . . . I realized that the first *question* to come up was: What has it meant to be a woman? *At first I thought I could dispose of that pretty quickly.* I had never had any feeling of inferiority, no one had ever said to me: "You think that way because you're a woman"; my femininity had

never been irksome to me in any way. "For me," I said to Sartre, "you might almost say it just hasn't counted." "All the same, you weren't brought up in the same way as a boy would have been: you should look into it further." *I looked and it was a revelation;* this world was a masculine world, my childhood had been nourished by myths forged by men. . . . I was so interested in this discovery that *I abandoned my project for a personal confession* in order to give all my attention to finding out about the condition of woman in general.

I described how [*The Second Sex*] was first conceived: almost by chance. Wanting to talk about myself, I became aware that to do so I should first have to describe the condition of woman in general; first, I considered the myths that men have forged about her through all their cosmologies, religions, superstitions, ideologies and literature. I tried to establish some order in the picture which at first appeared to me completely incoherent. (94, my emphasis)

Once the theoretical endeavor is engaged, however, once the confession is resisted, "Re-Vision" becomes as unavoidable as it is utterly surprising. The theorist in turn becomes a *witness* who cannot but testify, henceforth, to her own re-vision and her own experience of surprise: "I began to look at women with new eyes and found surprise after surprise lying in wait for me. It is both strange and stimulating to discover suddenly, after forty, an aspect of the world that has been staring you in the face all the time which somehow you have never noticed" (185).

The Resistance to Autobiography: Virginia Woolf

Strangers are an endangered species

In Emily Dickinson's house in Amherst
cocktails are served   the scholars
gather in celebration
their pious or clinical legends
festoon the walls like imitations
of period patterns

(. . . and, as I feared, my "life" was made a "victim")
The remnants pawed   the relics
the cult assembled in the bedroom

and you   whose teeth were set on edge by churches
resist your shrine
                              escape
                                          are found
nowhere
                    unless in words   (your own)

—ADRIENNE RICH, "The Spirit of Place"

Nothing could be further from the personality—and the persona—of Simone de Beauvoir than Virginia Woolf. De Beauvoir got the best French academic education, graduated from
the Sorbonne, and was ranked "second" (second best) in the
whole of France in the national *concours* (top-level educational
tests and competition) of the *Agrégation* (Sartre having been
ranked "first"). De Beauvoir thus utilized the best available educational resources in France and successfully competed with the
opportunities of men. Virginia Woolf, in contrast to Beauvoir
and in contrast also to her own father and brothers, was deprived
of college education and of the stimulus of academic striving.
"Still," writes Woolf ironically in a discussion on and in *A Room of
One's Own*,

> Still, you may object, why do you attach so much importance to
> this writing of books by women when, according to you, it re-
> quires so much effort, . . . and may bring one into very grave
> disputes with certain very good fellows? My motives, let me ad-
> mit, are partly selfish. *Like most uneducated Englishwomen, I like
> reading*—I like reading books in the bulk. Lately my diet has
> become a trifle monotonous; history is too much about wars;
> biography too much about great men; poetry has shown, I think, a
> tendency to sterility, and fiction—but I have sufficiently exposed
> my disabilities as a critic of modern fiction and will say no more
> about it. (112–13, my emphasis)

Yet, in spite of their differences of education, background, tem-
perament, and culture, Virginia Woolf proposes to combine, very

like Simone de Beauvoir, critical theory with literature, "philosophy" with "fiction": "I am by no means confining you to fiction. . . . For books have a way of influencing each other. Fiction
will be much the better for standing cheek by jowl with poetry
and philosophy" (113).

In much the same way as, for Simone de Beauvoir, autobiography is necessarily resisted—and necessarily inhabited—first by
theory and then by literature, for Virginia Woolf, in turn, though
in a reverse direction, theory is necessarily resisted—and necessarily inhabited—both by fiction (literature) and by a narrative
(autobiography) that, paradoxically, *gets personal* only in the way
in which it claims to be inherently *impersonal*. Invited to deliver
an academic lecture—a theoretical address—about "women and
fiction," Woolf starts by interrupting and disrupting her own
theoretical authority by a self-reference to an *I* which, while
subverting the impersonality of theory as a claim to universal
truth, introduces voice—a female voice—as the embodiment of
the singularity of a speaking subject and as the necessity of narrating, in effect, the autobiographical itinerary of that female voice
and of that woman speaker:

> But, you may say, we asked you to speak about women and
> fiction—what has that got to do with a room of one's own? I will
> try to explain. (4)

> And to answer that question I had to *think myself out of the room,
> back into the past.* (11)

> At any rate, when a subject is highly controversial—and any ques-
> tion about sex is that—one cannot hope to tell the truth. One can
> only show how one came to hold whatever opinion one does hold.
> One can only give one's audience the chance of drawing their own
> conclusions as they observe the limitations, the prejudices, the
> idiosyncrasies of the speaker. *Fiction here is likely to contain more
> truth than fact. Therefore I propose, making use of all the liberties and
> licenses of a novelist,* to *tell you the story* of the two days that preceded
> my coming here—how, bowed down by the weight of the subject
> you have laid upon my shoulders, I pondered it, and *made it work in
> and out of my daily life.* (4, my emphasis)

Through the insistence of the narrative *I*, autobiography[27] is summoned, then, as a *resistance to theory* and to its claim to be a statement and not merely an utterance—to be removed, that is, both from the *I* and from the circumstances and the process of its own origination. But at the same time, Woolf suggests the impossibility of a direct access to the female autobiography that she invokes, the necessary *detour of autobiography through fiction*, or through the rhetoric of literature: "Fiction here is likely to contain more truth than fact. . . . *I need not say that what I am about to describe has no existence;* Oxbridge is an invention; . . . *"I" is only a convenient term for somebody who has no real being*" (4). Literature, or fiction, is thus pointed to as autobiographical to the precise extent that it *resists* direct autobiography.

III

The Voice of What Cannot Be Named, or the *I* as Missing

But through this self-resistance inherent to *A Room of One's Own* and to the interaction it produces between theory, literature, and autobiography, female autobiography is implicitly presented from the start as profoundly problematic. The female speaker speaks from an autobiographical position that is defined as what cannot be simply named, or what can be named only as, precisely, nameless, missing:

> Here then was I (call me Mary Beton, Mary Seton, Mary Carmichael or by any name you please—it is not a matter of any importance). (5)

It might not be a matter of any importance. But who, in fact, does Virginia Woolf here *name* as the bearer of the *I*? It is doubtless no coincidence that this series of apparently gratuitous names replicates quite literally the lyrical succession of names in the last stanza of a well-known Scottish ballad:

Last night there were four Marys
Tonight there'll be but three
There was Mary Beton, and Mary Seton
And Mary Charmichael and me.

The ballad, which takes place in the sixteenth century in the court of Mary Stuart, Queen of Scots, is entitled "Mary Hamilton": it names thus "the fourth Mary," the one whose story it narrates and who, at the closure of the ballad, refers to herself as "me." A kitchen maid in the royal court, she bore an illegitimate son to the king, killed her own baby, and was executed by the queen. The ballad, spoken (sung) in her own voice, tells the story of her execution.

Word is to the kitchen gone
And word is to the hall
And word is up to Madam the Queen,
And that's the worst of all,
That Mary Hamilton's borne a babe
To the highest Stewart of all.

Arise, arise, Mary Hamilton,
Arise and tell to me
What thou hast done with thy wee babe
I saw and heard weep by thee.

"I put him in a tiny boat
And cast him out to sea
That he might sink or he might swim
But he'd never come back to me."

Arise, arise, Mary Hamilton,
Arise and come with me.
There is a wedding in Glasgow town
This night we'll go and see.

She put not on her robes of black
Nor her robes of brown.
But she put on her robes of white
To ride into Glasgow town.

And as she rode into Glasgow town
The city for to see
The bailiff's wife and the provost's wife
Cried, "Ach and alas for thee!"

"Ah, you need not weep for me," she cried.
"You need not weep for me.
For had I not slain my own wee babe
This death I would not dee [die].

"Ah little did my mother think
When first she cradled me
The lands I was to travel in
And the death I was to dee.

"Last night I washed the Queen's feet
And put the gold in her hair
And the only reward I find for this
The gallows to be my share."

"Cast off, cast off my gown," she cried,
"But let my petticoat be
And tie a napkin round my face
The gallows I would not see."

Then by and come the King himself
Looked up with a pitiful eye
"Come down, come down, Mary Hamilton,
Tonight you'll dine with me."

"Ah, hold your tongue, my sovereign liege,
And let your folly be
For if you'd a mind to save my life
You'd never have shamed me here.

"Last night there were four Marys
Tonight there'll be but three
There was Mary Beton, and Mary Seton,
And Mary Carmichael and me."

The Desire of the Patriarch

The nameless *I* who, present as an absence, is the bearer of the silence and the speech of *A Room of One's Own* and who, from within Woolf's text, addresses us with the enigma of its fictionality and of its autobiographical reality ("fiction here is likely to contain more truth than fact") is, therefore, the voice of a woman who is speaking insofar as she is *voiceless*, executed, dead. The repetition of the name of *Mary* is evocative of the myth of woman as at once a virgin and a mother. But Mary Hamilton, ironically enough, is neither properly a virgin (having been sexually exploited by the king) nor properly a mother (having killed her baby).

The ballad dramatizes, in this way, a primal scene of guilt that proceeds, in fact, from the father's (or the patriarch's, the king's) sin, but in which the woman, insofar as she acknowledges that her essence is to be a mother,[28] takes upon herself the guilt[29] and in effect condemns herself to death in almost welcoming her execution.

> "Ah, you need not weep for me," she cried.
> "You need not weep for me.
> For had I not slain my own wee babe
> This death I would not dee [die].
>
> "Ah little did my mother think
> When first she cradled me
> The lands I was to travel in
> And the death I was to dee."

The Mother's Story

"For we think back through our mothers if we are women," writes Virginia Woolf in *A Room of One's Own* (79), "—our mothers who found it difficult to scrape together thirty thousand pounds, our mothers who bore thirteen children to ministers of religion at St. Andrews" (24):

Making a fortune and bearing thirteen children—no human being could stand it. . . . First there are nine months before the baby
is born. Then there are three or four months spent in feeding the
baby. After the baby is fed there are certainly five years spent in
playing with the baby. . . . Moreover, it is equally useless to ask
what might have happened if Mrs. Seton and her mother and her
mother before her had amassed great wealth . . . because, in the
first place, to earn money was impossible for them, and in the
second, had it been possible, the law denied them the right to
possess what money they earned. . . . It would have been [their
husbands'] property. . . .

   At any rate, . . . there could be no doubt that . . . our mothers
had mismanaged their affairs very gravely. (22–23)

Only, if Mrs Seton and her like had gone into business at the age
of fifteen, there would have been—that was the snag in the
argument—no Mary. What, I asked, did Mary think of that? (22)

> Arise, arise, Mary Hamilton,
> Arise and tell to me
> What thou hast done with thy wee babe
> I saw and heard weep by thee.
>
> "I put him in a tiny boat
> And cast him out to sea
> That he might sink or he might swim
> But he'd never come back to me."

If Mary Hamilton rejects, thus, the maternal function, she can
assert herself only through death, articulate her story only by
taking upon herself the guilt of her own oppression by the patriarchal scene by welcoming her execution, by suicidally adhering
to her own destruction. Mary Hamilton's autobiography, in other words, is the story of her dispossession from her own autobiography.

   In contrast to Mary Hamilton, "Mary's mother"—and, we
might add, Virginia's mother—has accepted motherhood, or else
"there would have been no Mary"—and no Virginia. But mothers live, as mothers, through and for the story of the Other. The

story of the mother—that of Mrs. Ramsay in *To the Lighthouse*, that of Virginia's mother—is precisely one of having *no autobiography*, no story of her own.

> Only she thought life—and a little strip of time presented itself to her eyes—her fifty years. There it was before her—life. Life, she thought, but did not finish her thought. She took a look at life, for she had a clear sense of it there, something real, something private, which she shared neither with her children nor with her husband. A sort of transaction went on between them, in which *she was on one side, and life was on another*, and she was always trying to get the better of it, as it was of her.[30]

A Legacy of Death

"A woman writing thinks back through her mothers," insists the author of *A Room of One's Own* (101). In the case of Virginia's mother as in that of Mary Hamilton, however, the legacy of motherhood is not merely that of a life giver but, equally, a legacy of death.[31] Marked by the trauma of the early loss of her own mother, Virginia Woolf can think back through her mother autobiographically only insofar as her mother is herself, like Mary Hamilton, in essence a *dead* mother—dead as a result of fulfilling only too perfectly what Balzac might well have called "her woman's duty":[32]

> Despite her charities and her maternal commitments, Julia lived chiefly for her husband; everyone needed her but he needed her most. With his temperament and his necessities this was too great a task for even the most heroic of wives. . . .
> Beautiful still, but increasingly worn and harassed, Julia became more and more obsessed by time. She was always in a hurry, ever more anxious to save time by doing things herself, ever more anxious that others should be spared. And so she exhausted herself. Still young in years, *she had raced through a lifetime in altruistic work and at length her physical resistance burnt out.*[33]

Her mother, who holds her in her lap in her earliest memory, continues to dominate Virginia's memories of childhood. According to Leslie's reverential account of her, *to love was her essence*, and all her energies were spent in caring for other people. . . . Her mother's death—reinforced by [her sister] Stella's death two years later—was the cataclysmic disruption of [Virginia's] childhood.[34]

Autobiographically, Virginia Woolf can think back through her mother only insofar as her own life—and her own birth—is constituted by her mother's *split from her own autobiography*, and by her mother's death.

She Will Be Born

I have said that a woman writing thinks back through her mothers. Again if one is a woman one is often surprised by a sudden *splitting off of consciousness*, . . . when from being the natural inheritor of that civilization, she becomes, on the contrary, outside of it, alien and critical. (*A Room of One's Own*, 101)

As a corollary to the missing link in the chain of generations, the "splitting off of consciousness" is thus itself thought back through "the dark core" of the mother, through the black hole of her death and of the absence of her story.

It is, indeed, a different process of en-gendering that Virginia Woolf herself is now involved in, in trying—through the interaction between theory, literature, and her own life—to *give precisely birth* to Mary Hamilton as woman writer, and to "Shakespeare's sister" not merely as a female genius but as a *writer of Woolf's own autobiography*; an autobiography that, not by chance, encompasses *insanity and suicide* as the figures of its own impossibility and of its own annihilation; an autobiography that is therefore unwritable except through the story of the Other, but that succeeds precisely in inscribing *woman's split as groundbreaking*: as the groundbreaking process of a woman thinking—thinking back and thinking forward—through her own split.

This may be true or it may be false—who can say?—but what is true in it, so it seemed to me, reviewing the story of Shakespeare's sister as I had made it, is that any woman born with a great gift in the sixteenth century would certainly have *gone crazed, shot herself,* or ended her days in some lonely cottage outside the village, *half witch, half wizard. . . .* For it needs little skill in psychology to be sure that a highly gifted girl who had tried to use her gift for poetry would have been so thwarted and hindered by other people, so tortured and pulled asunder by her own contrary instincts, that *she must have lost her health and sanity to a certainty.* (*A Room of One's Own,* 51)

Through Shakespeare's sister, Woolf unwittingly thinks forward to her own autobiography and thinks back to a feminine biography in her own likeness.

I told you in the course of this paper that Shakespeare had a sister, but do not look for her in Sir Sidney Lee's Life of the Poet. *She died young*—alas, she never wrote a word. (*A Room of One's Own,* 117)

But in engendering uncannily, out of this literary story of the Other, her own impossible autobiography, in endowing Mary Hamilton with her own voice and Shakespeare's sister with her own unwritable life text, Virginia Woolf transforms her own insanity and suicide into *vehicles of writing* and into the inadvertent *speaking subjects* of a new mode of appeal and of a new structure—and a new power—of address:

> *With whom do you believe your lot is cast?*
> *From where does your strength come?*

Indeed, with whom do you believe your lot is cast? In the stories of this book, Balzac's Stéphanie in "Adieu," very much like Shakespeare's sister or Virginia Woolf, in turn "loses her health and sanity to a certainty": through her inadvertent feminine resistance to her so-called "woman's duty"—her role of serving as a mirror for her male companion—she too "goes crazed" and eventually "dies young." Balzac's Paquita in "The Girl with the Golden Eyes," in much the same way as Virginia Woolf, loves both a woman and a man, and for this double love as well for her resistance to sexual appropriation, she too pays with her life. In resisting Freud's "solution" Irma, in Freud's *Interpretation of Dreams*, would not be cured and is thus destined, again like Virginia Woolf, to remain ill.

Virginia Woolf writes:

Here then was I (call me Mary Beton, Mary Seton, Mary Charmichael or by any name you please . . .)

Could she not just as well have said: "Call me Stéphanie. . . . Call me Paquita. . . . Call me Irma. . . ."?

And yet Stéphanie, Paquita, Irma, Mary Hamilton are all renamed, rewritten, and in fact reborn through the testimonial speech act of Virginia Woolf's autobiographical, and literary, and theoretical pronouncement, "Here then was I," and through the power of address summoned by this speech act.

> With the hands of a daughter I would cover you
> from all intrusion   even my own
> saying   rest to your ghost
>
> with the hands of a sister I would leave your hands
> open or closed as they prefer to lie
> and ask no more of who or why or wherefore
>
> with the hands of a mother I would close the door
> on the rooms you've left behind
> and silently pick up my fallen work.[35]

I told you in the course of this paper that Shakespeare had a sister, but do not look for her in Sir Sidney Lee's life of the poet. *She died young*—alas, she never wrote a word. . . . Now my belief is that this poet who never wrote a word and who was buried at the crossroads still lives. She lives in you and in me, and in many other women who are not here tonight, for they are washing up the dishes and putting the children to bed. But she lives; for great poets do not die; . . . they need only the opportunity to walk among us in the flesh. This opportunity, as I think, it is now coming within your power to give her. For my belief is that if we live another century or so . . . if we face the fact, for it is a fact, that there is no arm to cling to, but that we go alone and that our relation is to the world of reality and not only to the world of men and women, then the opportunity will come and the dead poet who was Shakespeare's sister will put on the body which she has so often laid down. Drawing her life from the lives of the unknown who were her forerunners, . . . *she will be born.* (*A Room of One's Own,* 117–18)

The story of Virginia Woolf's impossible autobiography thus becomes not just the story of Shakespeare's sister's "loss of health and sanity to a certainty," but the narrative of the survival of a woman's writing and of the resistance of her *writer's certainty* even to the loss of health and life. It is at once this loss and this resistance that are transmitted to us through the bond of reading, and that continue to solicit us with their ongoing power to address and to engender. For when a woman's life—and death—is written in this way, we can be certain, in effect, that "we dead" can henceforth "awaken" to the *birth*, precisely, of our own auto-biography.

Notes

Chapter 1. What Does a Woman Want?

1. Adrienne Rich, *Of Woman Born: Motherhood as Experience and as Institution* (New York: Norton, 1976; Tenth Anniversary Edition, 1986), xxxii; my emphasis.

2. Sigmund Freud, letter to Marie Bonaparte, quoted in Ernest Jones, *The Life and Work of Sigmund Freud* (New York: Basic Books, 1955), 2:421.

3. Honoré de Balzac, "Adieu (Nouvelles philosophiques)," in *Le Colonel Chabert, suivi de El Verdugo, Adieu et Le Réquisitionnaire*, Collection "Folio" (Paris: Gallimard, 1974), 141–209; and "La Fille aux yeux d'or: The Girl with the Golden Eyes," in *History of the Thirteen*, trans. Herbert J. Hunt (Baltimore: Penguin, 1974), 307–91.

4. Sigmund Freud, "The Method of Interpreting Dreams: An Analysis of a Specimen Dream," in *The Interpretation of Dreams* (London: Hogarth Press, 1978), 96–121. Vol 4 of *The Standard Edition of the Complete Psychological Works of Sigmund Freud*, ed. and trans. James Strachey.

5. This is a quintessential, simplifying, schematizing summary of an interpretation that each chapter will develop in an infinitely deeper, more concrete, and more nuanced way.

6. Judith Fetterley, *The Resisting Reader: A Feminist Approach to American Fiction* (Bloomington: Indiana University Press, 1977), xii.

7. Adrienne Rich, "When We Dead Awaken: Writing as Re-Vision," in *On Lies, Secrets and Silence* (New York: Norton, 1979), 35.

8. For a lengthier elaboration of this conception of literature ("la chose littéraire"), see my *Writing and Madness: Literature/Philosophy/Psychoanalysis* (Ithaca, N.Y.: Cornell University Press, 1985), esp. 11–32 and 251–55, and *The Literary Speech Act* (Ithaca, N.Y.: Cornell Univer-

sity Press, 1983). See also the chapter "Psychoanalysis and Education: Teaching Terminable and Interminable" in my *Jacques Lacan and the Adventure of Insight: Psychoanalysis in Contemporary Culture* (Cambridge, Mass.: Harvard University Press, 1987), esp. 91–97, and the definition of literature proposed in the conclusion of my essay, "Turning the Screw of Interpretation," in *Literature and Psychoanalysis: The Question of Reading— Otherwise*, ed. S. Felman (Baltimore: Johns Hopkins University Press, 1977), a definition whose elaboration is introduced as follows: "There are *letters* from the moment there is no Master to receive them, or to *read* them: letters exist because a Master ceases to exist. We could indeed advance this statement as a definition of literature itself" (see development, pp. 206–7).

Other theorists and critics have, moreover, in their turn, though in different contexts, underscored a similar conception, equally central to their own specific critical endeavors. Among recent works, see for instance, Ross Chambers's explicitly political use of the concept, *literary discourse*, in his subtle analysis of what he calls "oppositional narrative" in *Room for Maneuver* (Chicago: University of Chicago Press, 1991), 3. ("Without falling into idealism, it is possible, I believe, to argue that discourse—and notably the discourse called literary—has characteristics that enable it, in an important sense, to elude both repression and recuperation, or more accurately to 'maneuver' within the 'room' that opens up *between* the two"), and Michel de Certeau's philosophical use of the concept, *fiction*, in his powerful reflection on the relation among history, psychoanalysis, and institutions in *Heterologies: Discourse on the Other* (Minneapolis: University of Minnesota Press, 1986), 202 ["Fiction plays on the stratification of meaning: it narrates one thing in order to tell something else; it delineates itself in a language from which it continuously draws effects of meaning that cannot be circumscribed or checked. . . . It is 'metaphoric'; it moves elusively in the domain of the other. Knowledge is insecure when dealing with the problem of fiction; consequently, its effort consists in an analysis (of a sort) that reduces or translates the elusive language of fiction into stable and easily combined elements"]).

9. See, in conjunction with the treatment by this chapter of the question of madness in its relation to women, my discussion of the controversy between Foucault and Derrida on the question of madness, its philosophical status, and its relation to the history of philosophy, in chapter 1 of my *Writing and Madness*, 33–55.

10. See my *Jacques Lacan and the Adventure of Insight*, esp. chap. 5, "Beyond Oedipus: The Specimen Story of Psychoanalysis," 98–159.

11. De Certeau, *Heterologies*, 199, emphasis mine.

12. Rich, "When We Dead Awaken," 35.

13. The word *resistance* is here used with a deliberate conflation of its various—and heterogeneous—connotations: physical, psychoanalytical, political, and ethical.

14. Simone de Beauvoir, *The Second Sex*, ed. and trans. H. M. Parshley (New York: Vintage, 1989), vii, x, emphasis mine.

15. In the 1982 film on Simone de Beauvoir produced by Malka Ribowska and José Dayan.

16. See Nancy Miller, *Getting Personal* (New York: Routledge, 1991) for a subtly nuanced feminist position that identifies, however, the autobiographical with the personal and the confessional. Miller points to the contemporary "outbreak of self-writing," which "(although it is not practiced uniquely by feminists or women) can be seen to develop out of feminist theory's original emphasis on the analysis of the personal: . . . the current proliferation in literary studies of autobiographical or personal criticism," and comments:

> The spectacle of a significant number of critics getting personal in their writing, while not, to be sure, on the order of a paradigm shift, is at least the sign of a turning point in the history of critical practices. . . . In the face of the visible extremes of racism or misogyny, or the equally violent silences of theoretical discourses from which all traces of embodiment have been carefully abstracted, the autobiographical project might seem a frivolous response. How can I propose a reflection about an ethics in criticism . . . from these individualistic grounds? But the risk of a limited personalism, I think, is a risk worth taking. ("Preface," *Feminist Confessions*, ix–x, xiv)

This equation between the autobiographical and the "confessional" is commonly encountered in current feminist criticism and perception. See, for instance, the excellent introduction of the editors to the section, "Autobiography," in the anthology entitled *Feminisms*: "When the writer's presence seems to tear through the fabric of the academic text—revealing glimmers of the lived experience that forms the context for scholarly writing—'confessional' moments occur in otherwise conventional prose. . . . The confessional mode can also govern an entire essay. . . . In this new form of academic writing, autobiography merges with scholarship, and a personal voice begins—if only tentatively—to take shape in expository prose" (Robyn R. Warhol and Diane Price Herndl, eds., *Feminisms: An Anthology of Literary Theory and Criticism* [New Brunswick, N.J.: Rutgers University Press, 1991], 1033).

For a different perspective, which insists on analyzing, on the contrary, the radical gap and consequent differentiation between "the autobiographical" and the illusions of the personal, see (in the same anthology) Shari Benstock's study of Virginia Woolf ("Authorizing Autobiography") and its critique of what might be called the mystique of traditional autobiography ("definitions of autobiography that stress self-disclosure and narrative account"), insofar as this tradition gravitates around the delusion of a coherent (or "organic") self. In contrast to this mystique, says Benstock, the modern feminine autobiographical project (as embodied by Virginia Woolf) stresses language as "a principle of separation and division" through which the "self" is at the same time constructed and decentered: "'Writing the self' is therefore a process of simultaneous sealing and splitting that can *only trace fissures of discontinuity*. This process may take place through 'the individual's special, peculiar psychic configuration,' but it is never an act of 'consciousness' pure and simple" (ibid., 1054, emphasis mine).

17. My point here is different from the one developed by Carolyn Heilburn in her moving and effective essay, *Writing a Woman's Life* (New York: Ballantine Books, 1988). Heilburn argues that women have been hindered in their quest for accomplishment because "power and control" have always been "declared unwomanly." As a result, "women have been deprived of the narratives, or the texts, plots, or examples, by which they might assume power over—take control of—their own lives" (17). "Power is the ability to take one's place in whatever discourse is essential to action and the right to have one's part matter" (18). Thus, women suffer from the fact that they have "no models on which to form their lives" (25). Heilburn's enterprise is to provide new models in narrating the life stories of exceptional women and in attempting to "face systematically" the "choices and pain of the women who did not make a man the center of their lives" (31), women who wrote themselves a "life beyond convention" (96) and thereby contributed to "transform female destiny" (120) and to create, specifically, "new stories" (122), having "moved beyond the categories our available narratives have provided for women" (131).

My argument is that *our own autobiography is not available to us*, not simply because we have no models and because, inhabiting male plots, we are enjoined not to transgress convention and to leave the realm of accomplishment to men (to live around a male center) but because we cannot simply *substitute ourselves as center* without regard to the *decentering* effects of language and of the unconscious, without acute awareness of the fact that our own relation to a linguistic frame of reference is never self-transparent. We can neither simply "write" our stories nor decide to write "new" stories, because we *do not know* our stories, and because the decision to "rewrite" them is not simply external to the language that unwittingly writes us. My emphasis is on the unavailability for women, not simply of "power" but of knowledge, and self-knowledge; on the unavailability, that is, not only of new models but of new linguistic *structures of address.*

The question of a model is one of origins, of sources. The question of address is one of goals, of destinations. Life as a complex relation to the Other (to society, to history) poses not merely the question, "What model do I imitate?" "What structure of otherness do I identify myself with?" but also, "What structure of otherness do I address myself to (in my speeches and my actions)?"

This is why the key, in my perspective, is in *learning how to read* (rhetorical, psychoanalytical, political, ethical) *structures of address* and in attempting, through the reading, to transform or "rewrite" these structures not merely from the vantage point of *one* language (in whose ethnocentric, pseudotransparent medium we will simply substitute one center for another, in shifting from male-centered plots to female-centered stories) but from the *cross-cultural* perspective of the difference and the interaction between different languages and cultures.

For a study of autobiography that insists, precisely, on a multicultural, multiracial, multilinguistic perspective, and yet that tries to analyze how women writers from different races and different languages, those specifically "who must survive (and write) in the interval between different cultures and languages," nonetheless share not just conflicts and dilemmas but common concerns, strategies, and ways of coping, see Françoise Lionnet, *Autobiographical Voices: Race, Gender, Self-Portraiture* (Ithaca: Cornell University Press, 1989).

18. Vita Sackville-West's autobiography was, as is well known, edited and published by her son, Nigel Nicolson, as *Portrait of a Marriage* (London: Weidenfeld and Nicolson, 1973 [citation from p. 9]). Vita's story, which she herself condemned to the *absence of a story* because she could not find in herself the force to address and to transmit it and because she literally locked it up and hid it, could thus accede to us, ironically only posthumously and distortedly, through the male intrusion of the son's voice and through the male-centered perspective of the son's own appropriation of the narrative in his framing, overseeing plot (turning the "writing of a woman's life" into the "portrait of a marriage").

19. Marguerite Duras, *La Douleur* (Paris: P.O.L., 1985), 10, my translation from the French.

20. See Laura S. Brown, "Not Outside the Range: One Feminist Perspective on Psychic Trauma," in *Psychoanalysis, Culture and Trauma,* ed. Cathy Caruth (*American Imago* 48, no. 1 [1991]). Discussing the traditional psychiatric (diagnostic) definition of "psychic trauma,"

Brown argues that "the notion that [traumatic] events must be 'outside the range of human experience' in order to qualify as traumatic stressors results in excluding many traumatic events that are common in the lives of girls and women" (110). Brown refers not only to the great numbers, among women, of abuse, rape, and incest survivors but to the "traumatic stressors" involved in "all those everyday, repetitive, interpersonal events that are so often the sources of psychic pain for women" and to the unconscious transmission from generation to generation of those "insidious traumata": "How, then, do we understand the woman whose symptoms of psychic trauma have occurred entirely at second hand, as it were, through the mechanism of insidious trauma? Mainstream trauma theory has begun to recognize that post-traumatic symptoms can be intergenerational, as in the case of children of survivors of the Nazi Holocaust; we have yet to admit that it can be spread laterally throughout an oppressed social group . . . for whom insidious trauma is a way of life" (128–29).

On the transmission of trauma from generation to generation, see Dori Laub's moving and illuminating theoretical, clinical, and autobiographical insights in chapters 2 and 3 of Shoshana Felman and Dori Laub, M.D., *Testimony: Crises of Witnessing in Literature, Psychoanalysis and History* (New York: Routledge, 1992), 57–92.

21. For a comprehensive definition of trauma in both its psychoanalytical and philosophical significance, and specifically in its relation to memory, see Cathy Caruth's introduction to *Psychoanalysis, Culture, and Trauma* (*American Imago* 48, no. 1 [1991], no. 4 [1992]).

22. It is not that women do not have the possibility, or the right, to *confess* their stories. The critical fashion of autobiographical confession among feminist writers attests to the contrary and has its important critical reasons. But female autobiography, I am suggesting, is not *available* to a confession and cannot truly and effectively be accessed by this mode, which, in its inadvertent search for absolution (the originary and, in fact, the inescapable desire behind any confession), runs the risk of offering still more masks (idealizing or counteridealizing) for a self-conscious feminine identity still unwittingly preoccupied with exorcising female guilt, a perennial exercise that inexorably amounts (no matter how sincere and in good faith) to a false confession, or what I would call "*a screen confession,*" in the sense I use when I refer (in chap. 4, on Balzac's "The Girl with the Golden Eyes") to the textual functioning of "*a screenwoman,*" or in the sense Freud uses in speaking of "screen memories."

23. See Laub, "Truth, Testimony, and Survival," in Felman and Laub, *Testimony,* chap. 3, 75–92.

24. See my "The Return of the Voice: Claude Lanzmann's *Shoah,*" in Felman and Laub, *Testimony,* chap. 7, 204–83.

25. Bell Hooks, "Writing Autobiography," from *Talking Back: Thinking Feminist, Thinking Black* in Warhol and Hernde, *Feminisms*, 1036.

26. Rich, "When We Dead Awaken," 48, 35, 139.

Chapter 2. Women and Madness

1. Phyllis Chesler, *Women and Madness* (Garden City, N.J.: Doubleday, 1973), xxii.

2. Luce Irigaray, *Speculum de l'autre femme* (Paris: Les Editions de Minuit, 1974); *Speculum of the Other Woman*, trans. Gillian Gill (Ithaca, N.Y.: Cornell UP, 1987).

3. Freud has thus pronounced his famous verdict on women: "Anatomy is destiny." But this is precisely the focus of the feminist contestation.

4. Honoré de Balzac, "Adieu" in *Colonel Chabert, suivi de El Verdugo, Adieu, et du Requisitionnaire*, edited and annotated by Philippe Berthier. Preface by Pierre Gascan (Paris: 1974).

5. Balzac, "Adieu," 9. Quotations from the Préface, the "Notice" and from Balzac's text are my translations; in all quoted passages, emphasis mine unless otherwise indicated.

6. Louis Althusser, *Lire le Capital* (Paris: F. Maspero, 1968), 1:26–28 (translation mine; emphasis Althusser's).

7. Balzac, "Adieu," 148, 156, 159, 164.

8. Michel Foucault, *Histoire de la folie à l'âge classique* (Paris: Gallimard, 1972), 540 (citations from Foucault are in my translation; page references are to the French original); *Madness and Civilization: A History of Insanity in the Age of Reason*, trans. Richard Howard (New York: Vintage Books, 1973).

9. This suicidal murder is, in fact, a repetition not only of Philippe's military logic and his attitude throughout the war scene but also of a specific previous moment in his relationship with Stéphanie. Well before the story's end, Philippe had already been on the point of killing Stéphanie, and himself with her, having, in a moment of despair, given up the hope of her ever recognizing him. The doctor, seeing through Philippe's intentions, had then saved his niece with a perspicacious lie, playing precisely on the specular illusion of her proper name. " 'You do not know then,' went on the doctor coldly, hiding his horror, 'that last night in her sleep she said, "Philippe!." ' 'She named me,' cried the baron, letting his pistols drop" (206).

10. Here again, the ambiguous logic of the "savior," in its tragic and heroic narcissism, is prefigured by the war scene. Convinced of his good reason, Philippe, characteristically, imposes it, by force, on others, so as to "save" them; but ironically and paradoxically, he always saves them *in*

spite of themselves: "'Let us save her in spite of herself!' cried Philippe, sweeping up the countess" (182).

11. Pierre Gascar, Preface to Balzac, "Adieu," 8.

Chapter 3. Textuality and the Riddle of Bisexuality

1. Sigmund Freud, "Femininity," in *New Introductory Lectures on Psychoanalysis*, trans. James Strachey (New York: Norton, 1965), 112.

2. Freud, Preface to *New Introductory Lectures*, 5.

3. Ibid., emphasis mine.

4. Honoré de Balzac, "La Fille aux yeux d'or," in *Histoire des Treize*. Citations are to: "The Girl with the Golden Eyes," in *History of the Thirteen*, trans. Herbert J. Hunt (Baltimore: Penguin, 1974). Where I have modified the English translation, the page reference is followed by the abbreviation TM (translation modified).

5. Unlike Henri, however, Paquita, in time, renounces her model of sexual hierarchization, her rhetorical subordination of the masculine to the feminine pole. In their second sexual encounter,

> "Put my velvet gown on me," said Henri coaxingly.
>
> "No, no" she impetuously replied. "*Remain what you are*, one of these angels I had been taught to detest and whom I looked upon only as monsters." (380, emphasis mine)

6. Freud, "The Uncanny," in *Sigmund Freud on Creativity and the Unconscious*, ed. and trans. Alix Strachey (New York: Harper Torchbooks, 1958), 148.

7. As the prologue indeed paternalistically affirms: "*quod erat demonstrandum*, if one may be permitted to apply a Euclidean formula to the science of manners" (327). What the "demonstration" consists of, however, is by no means clear.

8. See the remarkable article by Leyla Perrone-Moisès, "Le Récit euphémique," *Poétique*, no. 17 (1974).

Chapter 4. Competing Pregnancies

1. Juliet Mitchell, *Psychoanalysis and Feminism: Freud, Reich, Laing and Women* (New York: Vintage Books, 1975), xiii.

2. Jacques Lacan, "Une pratique de bavardage," *Ornicar?* No. 19 (1979), 5; my translation.

3. Betty Friedan, *The Second Stage* (New York: Summit Books, 1981).

4, See Betty Friedan, *The Feminine Mystique* (New York: Norton, 1974; New York: Dell, Laurel Books, 1982).

5. Sigmund Freud, letter to Marie Bonaparte, quoted in Ernest Jones, *The Life and Work of Sigmund Freud* (New York: Basic Books, 1955), 2:421.

6. Freud, "Femininity," in *New Introductory Lectures on Psycho-Analysis*, the Standard Edition of the Complete Psychological Works of Sigmund Freud, ed. and trans. James Strachey (London: Hogarth Press and the Institute of Psychoanalysis, 1964), 22:114.

7. See Freud's letter to Fliess on June 12, 1900 (Freud, Letter 137): Freud describes a visit to Bellevue, the house where he earlier had this dream. "Do you suppose," he writes, "that some day a marble tablet will be placed on the house, inscribed with these words?—

In this house, on July 24th, 1895
the secret of Dreams was Revealed
to Dr. Sigm. Freud

At the moment there is little prospect of it" (4:121). July 24, 1895, was the date of the Irma dream.

8. This has invariably been the feminist approach to the Irma dream. See in particular Monique Schneider, *La Parole et l'inceste* (Paris: Aubier-Montaigne, 1980) and Sarah Kofman, *L'Enigme de la femme* (Paris: Galilée, 1980), whose feminist rereadings of the dream I summarize and methodologically discuss in a later section of this essay. See also Mary Jacobus's use of the Irma dream in her perspicacious article, "Is There a Woman in This Text?" *New Literary History* 14 (Autumn 1982), 117–41. The demystifying posture with respect to Freud is by no means particular, however, to the feminist critics of Freud's work: it characterizes many psychoanalytic (or psychiatric) reinterpretations of the dream, such as: Max Schur, "Some Additional 'Day Residues' of 'The Specimen Dream of Psychoanalysis,'" in *Freud and His Self-Analysis*, edited by Mark Kanzer and Jules Glenn (New York: Jason Aronson, 1979), 87–116; R. Greenberg and C. Perlman, "If Freud Only Knew: A Reconsideration of Psychoanalytic Dream Theory," *International Review of Psychoanalysis* 5 (1978): 71–75; Adam Kuper and Alan A. Stone, "The Dream of Irma's Injection: A Structural Analysis," *American Journal of Psychiatry* 139 (Oct. 1982): 1125–34. In the last essay, the demystifying, condescending attitude toward Freud reaches its climactic point: "Freud censored any asso-

ciations to the dream that would have reflected adversely on Fliess and, in the place of what was censored, offered what we think are less relevant, even misleading, associations. Schur hypothesized that Freud's censorship was unconscious. Greenberg and Perlman accepted this hypothesis. . . . We disagree. . . . We believe . . . that Freud consciously and deliberately mislead his readers in order to conceal Fliess's involvement in the treatment" (1128).

In opposition to this (non-self-analytic) posture of critical condescension and epistemological superiority with respect to Freud ("Freud did not yet know that such protestations and negations stood for their opposite" [Schur, "Some Additional 'Day Residues,'" 1979], 98; "This solution was evident to us and not to Freud, Erikson, Schur and other commentators" [Kuper and Stone, "The Dream of Irma's Injection," 1233]), I would propose a type of textual approach that endorses Jacques Lacan's conception of an "ethics of psychoanalysis" that is also, among other things, an *ethics of interpretation:* an ethics of approach to the interpreted. "Inasmuch as it is out of the question," writes Lacan, "to psychoanalyze deceased authors, it is out of the question to psychoanalyze Freud's dream better than Freud himself. . . . What we can do is not supply an exegesis where Freud himself interrupts himself but rather take together [as an object for a new examination] the whole textual corpus of the dream and Freud's interpretation of the dream. There, we are in a *different position* than that of Freud." Jacques Lacan, "Le Rêve de l'injection d'Irma," in *Le Séminaire.* Bk. 2, *Le Moi dans la theorie de Freud et dans la technique de la psychanalyse* (Paris: Seuil, 1978), 183; my translation.

The interpretive claim of the reading endeavored here is thus not one of superiority (over Freud or any of his commentators) but (self-analytically, I hope) one of difference, of a different position (vantage point) with respect to the insight of Freud's text.

9. Life experience: Freud's as well as mine. For the reader is indeed invited to dream (and to interpret dreams) along with Freud: "And now," writes Freud, "I must ask the reader to make my interests his own for quite a while, and plunge, along with me, into the minutest details of my life; for a *transference* of this kind is peremptorily demanded by our interest in the hidden meaning of the dream." (4:105–6; my emphasis).

10. Pregnant, indeed, with Anna Freud.

11. Strachey's translation modified in accordance with Jane Gallop's correction. Jane Gallop, *The Father's Seduction* (Ithaca: Cornell University Press, 1982), 66.

12. Kate Millet, *Sexual Politics* (Garden City, N.Y.: Doubleday, 1969; New York: Avon Books, 1971). All citations are to the Avon edition.

13. I put "first stage" in quotation marks because it seems obvious to me that a feminist reflection—and a feminist position in concrete

existence—cannot simply coincide with a linear chronology, much less with a chronology of progress. The first stage is not simply necessary as a starting point: it can never be simply overcome, simply transcended; it *persists*, in fact, throughout the second (and the third) stage. Rather than a mere chronology, the metaphor of "stages" is a figure, here, for an increasingly nuanced perception—and account—of complexity. The stages, paradoxically, coexist.

14. Schneider, *La Parole et l'inceste*, 132. Translations of this work from the French are mine.

15. Erik Erikson, "The Dream Specimen of Psychoanalysis," *Journal of the American Psychoanalytic Association*, 2 (1954): 5–56. A summarized version of this reading is in E. Erikson, *Identity, Youth and Crisis* (New York: Norton, 1968). I use "DS" ("Dream Specimen") to refer to the longer essay and "IYC" ("Identity, Youth, Crisis") to refer to the book.

16. "*Trimethylamin*. I saw the chemical formula of this substance in my dream. . . . What was it, then to which my attention was to be directed in this way by trimethylamin? It was to a conversation with another friend who had for many years been familiar with all my writings during the period of their gestation, just as I had been with his. He had at the time confided some ideas to me on the subject of the chemistry of the sexual processes, and had mentioned among other things that he believed that one of the products of sexual metabolism was trimethylamin. Thus this substance led me to sexuality, the factor to which I attributed the greatest importance in the origin of the nervous disorders which it was my aim to cure. . . . I began to guess why the formula for trimethylamin had been so prominent in the dream. So many important substances converged upon that one word. Trimethylamin was an allusion not only to the immensely powerful factor of sexuality, but also to a person whose agreement I recalled with satisfaction whenever I felt isolated in my opinions" (4:116–17).

17. Kofman, *L'Enigme de la femme*, 55. Translations of this work from the French are mine.

18. See Edgar Allen Poe's short story "The Purloined Letter," J. Lacan's famous analysis of it entitled "Seminar on The Purloined Letter," in *Écrits* (New York: Norton, 1977), and my analysis of Lacan's interpretation in chapter 2 of my *Jacques Lacan and the Adventure of Insight: Psychoanalysis in Contemporary Culture*, 26–51.

19. See my essay, "Turning the Screw of Interpretation," in S. Felman, ed., *Literature and Psychoanalysis: The Question of Reading— Otherwise* (Baltimore: Johns Hopkins University Press, 1982), 201–3.

20. Strachey's translation here is modified in accordance with Erik Erikson's translation in DS 14.

21. See *The Interpretation of Dreams*, chap. 7: "Whereas the wish from

the *Ucs.* is able to find expression in the dream after undergoing distortions of every kind, the dominant system withdraws into a *wish to sleep*, realizes that wish by bringing about the modifications which it is able to produce in the cathexes within the psychical apparatus, and persists in that wish throughout the whole duration of sleep" (5:570; Freud's emphasis).

22. "Now that we know," writes Freud, "that all through the night the preconscious is concentrated upon the wish to sleep, we are in a position to carry our understanding of the process of dreams a stage further" (5:573). The dream's role is to be "a *guardian* of sleep" (5:580, Freud's emphasis).

23. Friedrich Nietzsche, *Thus Spoke Zarathustra* ("On the Teachers of Virtue"), in *The Portable Nietzscshe*, trans. Walter Kaufmann (New York: Viking Press, 1971), 142; translation modified.

24. "Irma's *complaint:* pains in the throat and abdomen and stomach; it was choking her" (4:109). "The still unexplained *complaint* about *pains* in the abdomen" (4:110).

25. J. Lacan, Kanzer Seminar, Yale University, 1975; trans. Barbara Johnson.

26. The feminist interpretations, incidentally, derive critically from Lacan's perspective. See J. Lacan, *Le Seminaire*, 2:177–204; also 2:150–52, 2:164–66.

Chapter 5. With Whom Do You Believe Your Lot Is Cast?

1. See Adrienne Rich, "Natural Resources," in *The Dream of a Common Language* (New York: Norton, 62):

> The phantom of the-man-who-would-understand
> the lost brother, the twin—
> . . . .
> did we invent him, conjure him . . .
> the man-who-would-dare-to-know-us?

2. Carol Gilligan, "Teaching Shakespeare's Sister: Notes from the Underground of Female Adolescence," in *Making Connections: The Relational Worlds of Adolescent Girls at Emma Willard School*, edited by Carol Gilligan, Nona Lyons, and Trudy Hanmer (Cambridge: Harvard University Press, 1990), 9–10.

3. In Audre Lorde, *Our Dead Behind Us* (New York: Norton, 1986), 61.

4. Heilburn, *Writing a Woman's Life*, 47.

5. Adrienne Rich, "Sources," in *Your Native Land, Your Life* (New York: Norton, 1986), 26.

6. Ibid., 6.

7. The question—and the verse—recurs both in "Sources" in *Your Native Land, Your Life* (see n. 5) and in "The Spirit of Place" in *A Wild Patience Has Taken Me This Far* (see n. 8).

8. Adrienne Rich, "The Spirit of Place," in *A Wild Patience Has Taken Me This Far* (New York: Norton, 1981), 41; first emphasis Rich's, second mine.

9. Rich, "When We Dead Awaken," 17–18, my emphasis.

10. Sackville-West, in Nicolson, *Portrait of a Marriage*, 9, emphasis mine.

11. For an unprecedented theoretical definition and concrete illustration of the vital importance (both historical and clinical) of "the internal witness" in the process of survival, see Laub, "Truth, Testimony and Survival," in *Testimony*, chapter 3.

12. See the testimony of Vita's son, Nigel Nicolson, in *Portrait of a Marriage*: "The effect of Vita on Virginia is all contained in *Orlando*, the longest and most charming love letter in literature" (201).

13. See Paul de Man, "The Resistance to Theory," in *The Resistance to Theory* (Minneapolis: University of Minnesota Press, 1986), 3–20.

14. In Shari Benstock's astute terms: see chap. 1, n. 16.

15. Adrienne Rich, *Of Woman Born: Motherhood as Experience and as Institution* (New York: Norton, 1976; Tenth Anniversary Edition, 1986), x, my emphasis.

16. Rich, "One Kind of Terror: A Love Poem," in *Your Native Land, Your Life* (New York: Norton, 1986), 55.

17. Stated two years earlier, in 1971, in "When We Dead Awaken: Writing as Re-Vision," in *On Lies, Secrets and Silence* (New York: Norton, 1979), 37–38; see my citation from, and my comments on, this theory, in chapter 1.

18. Rich, "Diving into the Wreck," in *Diving into the Wreck* (New York: Norton, 1973), 24, my emphasis.

19. Rich, "Coast to Coast," in *A Wild Patience Has Taken Me This Far* (New York: Norton, 1981), 6–7.

20. See Shoshana Felman and Dori Laub, M.D., "Foreword," *Testimony: Crises of Witnessing in Literature, Psychoanalysis, and History* (New York: Routledge, 1992), in which the authors propose a theory of "literature and art as a precocious mode of testimony—of accessing reality—when all other modes of knowledge are precluded" (xx).

21. Rich, "One Kind of Terror: A Love Poem," in *Your Native Land*, 53, my emphasis.

22. Rich, "Meditations for a Savage Child," in *Diving into the Wreck*, 57–58.

23. "I am really asking," writes Rich, "whether women cannot begin, at last, to *think through the body*, to connect with what has been so cruelly disorganized—our great mental capacities—hardly used; our highly developed tactile sense; our genius for close observation, our complicated, pain enduring, multi-pleasured physicality" (*Of Woman Born*, 284).

24. Rich, "When We Dead Awaken," 43.

25. Virginia Woolf, *A Room of One's Own* (New York: Harcourt Brace Jovanovich, 1957), 4.

26. Simone de Beauvoir, *Force of Circumstance*, trans. Richard Howard (New York: G. P. Putnam's Sons, 1964/1965), v, 94, my emphasis.

27. "I made it work in and out of my daily life"; "I had to think myself out of the room, and into the past."

28. For an echoing perception of motherhood as the idealized quintessence of womanhood, but seen from a male perspective, see later my analysis of the emergence of the figure of the mother in Freud's dreams and in Freud's theory of dreams in chapter 4, "Competing Pregnancies: The Dream from which Psychoanalysis Proceeds", especially the subsections entitled "Competing Pregnancies" and "The Navel of the Dream." For varying perspectives on the question of the mother as central to feminist reflection of the last decade, and on the controversy this question has sparked between the radical feminist view of "motherhood as the annihilation of women" (or at least of motherhood as the quintessence of women's powerlessness, of their definition from outside themselves, and of the control and exploitation of their bodies) and the revisionist feminist view of motherhood as, on the contrary, a unique experience of fulfillment and realization of women (but defined in new terms, within the framework of a renewed conception of the mother-child relation, and on the condition of a *recovery of the mother's own voice*, typically repressed and silenced in our culture), see, among others, Rich's classic, *Of Woman Born*; Nancy Chodorow, *The Reproduction of Mothering* (Berkeley and Los Angeles: University of California Press, 1978); the collaborative collections, *Mothering: Essays in Feminist Theory*, edited by Joyce Trebilcot (Totawa, N.J.: Rowman and Allanheld, 1983) and *The (M)other Tongue: Essays in Feminist Interpretation*, edited by Shirley Nelson Garner, Claire Kahane, and Madelon Sprengenther (Ithaca: Cornell University Press, 1985); Barbara Johnson, "My Monster/Myself" and "Apostrophe, Animation, and Abortion," in *A World of Difference* (Baltimore: Johns Hopkins University Press, 1987); Marianne Hirsch, *The Mother/Daughter Plot: Narrative, Psychoanalysis, Feminism* (Bloomington: Indiana University Press, 1989); Susan Rubin Suleiman, "Writing and

Motherhood," in *The (M)other Tongue*, "Feminist Intertextuality and the Laugh of the Mother," in *Subversive Intent: Gender, Politics, and the Avant-Garde* (Cambridge: Harvard University Press, 1990), 141–81, and "On Maternal Splitting," *Signs: Journal of Women in Culture and Society* 14, no. 1 (1988); Ann Willard, "Cultural Scripts for Mothering," in *Mapping the Moral Domain*, edited by Carol Gilligan, Janie Victoria Ward, and Jill McLean Taylor, with Betty Bardige (Cambridge: Harvard University Press, 1988); Julia Kristeva, "Stabat Mater," in *The Kristeva Reader*, edited by Toril Moi (Oxford: Basil Blackwell, 1986); Luce Irigaray, "When Our Lips Speak Together," trans. Carolyn Burke, *Signs*, no. 6 (Autumn 1980), 69–79, and "And the One Doesn't Stir without the Other," trans. Hélène Wenzel, *Signs*, no. 7 (Autumn 1981), 60–67.

29. On the guilt of the impossibility of being a mother or of living up to the mother's idealized role, and on the role of the mother, on the other hand, as a vehicle in the transmission of female guilt and female powerlessness (female self-condemnation and self-censorship) from one generation to another, see also my comments in chapter 1 on Vita Sackville-West's autobiography, and on the way this autobiography may have been destined, paradoxically, either to Vita's mother (as its censor) or to Vita's son (as its posthumous publisher: the son for whom she had to be—and could not adequately be—a mother).

30. Virginia Woolf, *To the Lighthouse* (New York: Harcourt Brace Jovanovich, 1955), 91–92, emphasis mine.

31. But "the void," writes Adrienne Rich, "is not something created by patriarchy, or racism, or capitalism. It will not fade with any of them. It is part of every woman.

"'The dark core,' *Virginia Woolf named it, writing of her mother.*" The dark core. It is beyond personality; beyond who loves or hates us" (*On Lies, Secrets, and Silence*, op. cit., p. 191).

And French psychoanalyst Luce Irigaray, looking in her turn into this unnameable "dark core" or this vertiginous maternal black hole, writes enigmatically, whether in her own voice or in the voice of women patients ("And the One Doesn't Stir without the Other," 66–67, my emphasis): "With your milk, Mother, you fed me ice. And if I leave, you lose the reflection of life, of your life. *And if I remain, am I not the guarantor of your death?* Each of us lacks her own image; her own face, the animation of her own body is missing. . . . *What I wanted from you, mother, was this: that in giving me life, you still remain alive.*" Virginia Woolf's mother did not.

The most original and most profound reflections I have encountered on this unsettling relationship between motherhood and death, and between female autobiography and the mother's death, are by Barbara Johnson, in her groundbreaking essays, on the one hand, on Mary Shelley's *Frankenstein* as an uncanny, "monstrous" autobiographical attempt deriving from the female autobiographer's originary loss of her own mother at her own birth ("My Monster/Myself") and, on the other hand, on female poems of abortion, an innovative female poetry that gives voice to, and explores, a less familiar (a tabooed?) figure of the bereaving mother living, and surviving, the "abortion," or the death of her own baby. See, for instance, a Mary Hamilton for the twentieth century, Gwendolyn Brooks's "The Mother" (*Selected Poems*, San Francisco: Harper and Row, 1963):

> Abortions will not let you forget,
> You remember the children you got that you did not get
> . . . .
> I have heard in the voice of the wind the voices of my dim killed
> children . . .
> . . . .
> If I poisoned the beginnings of your breaths
> Believe me that even in my deliberateness I was not deliberate
> . . . .
> Though why should I whine,
> Whine that the crime was other than mine?—
> Since anyhow you are dead.
> Or rather, or instead,
> You were never made.

Johnson points to the pathos of a new rhetoric of address implicit in these poems, in which the mother is not simply, as is usually the case in the male tradition, the one who is addressed (the object of a call, of an apostrophe) but rather herself the one who is addressing, the addressor, whereas the addressee is, unexpectedly, her dead (killed?) child (see "Apostrophe, Animation, and Abortion"). Both of these essays are in Barbara Johnson, *A World of Difference* (Baltimore: Johns Hopkins University Press, 1987).

32. This is the first title Balzac gave to the novella later entitled "Adieu."

33. Quentin Bell, *Virginia Woolf: A Biography* (New York: Harcourt Brace Janovich, 1972), 38–39, my emphasis.

34. Phyllis Rose, *Woman of Letters: Virginia Woolf* (New York: Harcourt Brace Jovanovich, 1978), 9–16, my emphasis.

35. Rich, "The Spirit of Place," in *A Wild Patience Has Taken Me This Far*, 43–45.

Index